▪ Backyard Play Areas You Can Make ▪

Complete Plans and Instructions for Building Playhouses, Forts, and Swing Sets

Paul Gerhards

STACKPOLE
BOOKS

Published by
STACKPOLE BOOKS
5067 Ritter Road
Mechanicsburg, PA 17055

Printed in the United States of America

Cover design by Caroline Miller
Cover photograph by Paul Gerhards

First Edition

10 9 8 7 6 5 4 3 2 1

Library of Congress Cataloging-in-Publication Data

Gerhards, Paul.
    Backyard play areas you can make : complete plans and instructions for building
    playhouses, forts, and swing sets / Paul Gerhards. — 1st ed.
        p.   cm.
    ISBN 0-8117-3088-3
    1. Playhouses, Children's—Design and construction. 2. Swings—Design and
    construction. I. Title.
TH4967.G47   1995
688. 7 '6—dc20
                                                                94-26961
                                                                    CIP

For my mother,
who believes a person is never too old for a playhouse

▪ Contents ▪

▪ Introduction ▪

When my mother was a little girl, her family moved into a house that had an old chicken coop in the backyard. My grandfather spent hours scrubbing down the chicken coop with lye soap. There was something magical about that lye soap, and when my grandfather finished, he presented my mother with a spanking clean playhouse. The once humble chicken coop had been transformed into a little girl's sanctuary and an incubator of her imagination.

Not too many homes these days come with chicken coops in their backyards. But with a few tools, readily available materials, a modicum of building skills, and this book, you can construct a respectable playhouse, fort, or swing set in your own backyard.

A playhouse can be much more than a place for children or grandchildren to play. For you, the builder, it can be a chance to try out new or sharpen old skills. If you've never built anything before, don't be intimidated. Study the information in this book. If necessary, seek the advice of local experts. Then plunge in.

Building a playhouse can be a rewarding challenge. And even if the finished product doesn't look like it would qualify for placement on the Street of Dreams, your children or grandchildren will find joy enough to compensate.

A playhouse can be as simple as a shed or as complex as a small home. You can build it with or without operable doors and windows. You can wire it for light and sound. You can panel, paint, or paper interior walls, carpet the floor, and fit the roof with a skylight. You can add window boxes and numerous other frills. What you can do with a playhouse is limited only by your imagination. My mother was right: You're never too old for a playhouse.

▪ PART I ▪

The Basics

This book showcases a number of ideas for playhouses and other backyard structures and presents them in a way that even readers with limited experience in building can construct a safe and attractive place for children to play. Part 1 consists of fundamentals based on conventional framing practices. They are general in nature and are not necessarily a step-by-step guide for any of the designs in particular. Information specific to each project follows in part 2.

For those knowledgeable in conventional building practices, this first section will provide little new information, and the plans themselves will be sufficient. There are, however, a few comments in part 1 regarding rough openings, windows, and doors that

might prove useful. Experienced carpenters know that there is more than one way to build almost anything. Methods and practices vary from one area to another, and often there is no one best way to accomplish a given task. I encourage the reader to adapt the plans and make use of other methods as seen fit. The most important concern is to maintain a high standard of safety by not compromising structural integrity.

Nearly every community has codes, restrictions, or other stipulations regarding the construction of many new structures. Before beginning a project, check with your local building department to learn of any requirements and obtain any necessary permits.

▪ Materials and Hardware ▪

DIMENSION LUMBER

Dimension lumber is used for general construction purposes and is referred to by nominal thickness and width, such as 2×4 or 2×6. A board's actual dimensions are generally ½ inch less than its nominal dimensions, although this may vary from one area to another.

Although pieces of dimension lumber are often referred to as boards, this term also refers collectively to 1× stock, such as 1×2, 1×4, or 1×6. These boards actually are ¾ inch thick and approximately ½ inch narrower than the nominal width given.

Dimension lumber is a softwood lumber milled from evergreens such as fir, pine, hemlock, cedar, or redwood. Fir, pine, and hemlock are the species generally used for framing, depending on the area. Cedar and redwood, because of their natural resistance to insects, rot, and disease, are used for exterior applications such as decks, railings, siding, and trim. Cedar and redwood may be left unfinished, but a good stain will enhance their beauty and prolong their life. Left untreated, redwood will turn black and cedar gray.

Lumber for framing comes in four grades: #1, select structural; #2, standard; #3, utility; and #4, economy.

Of these grades, standard and utility are more than adequate for framing the playhouses. For the play structures, standard and select (often referred to as standard and better and priced the same) are good choices. The better grades have fewer and tighter knots and no wanes. (A wane occurs when a board is milled with a slice of bark, which later falls away and leaves a void on an edge) Economy lumber is not recommended for any application described in this book.

All wood that comes in contact with or within 6 inches of the ground should be cedar, redwood, or pressure-treated (PT). Several manufacturers produce lumber specifically treated for deck construction and other outdoor applications. This is a good choice for framing members that will be embedded in or come close to the ground.

SHEET MATERIALS

Sheet materials include plywood, oriented strand board (OSB), particle board, hardboard, and other compressed wood products. These come in standard 4×8-foot sheets.

For years, ½-inch fir plywood was the standard sheathing material for residential construction. In many areas, however, plywood sheathing has been replaced by OSB. Sometimes called wafer board or waffle board, OSB is made of thousands of flakes of wood compressed into sheets $\frac{7}{16}$ inch thick and held together with waterproof resin.

Plywood comes in a variety of grades. The letters A through D designate the quality of each face, A being the best and D the worst. The letter X, as in CDX, indicates that the plywood is suitable for exterior applications. All fir plywood made today is glued together with waterproof resin.

Particle board (from ¼ to ¾ inch) can be used as floor underlayment (installed over the subfloor and under carpet, for example) and for walls. Particle board should not be allowed to get wet, as it will absorb water and break down quickly.

Materials commonly used in one area may be unavailable in another. The best advice on what material to use will come from your building materials supplier.

HARDWARE

You will need a variety of hardware items to construct any of the projects in this book.

Most of the hardware is for fastening one piece to another. The primary fastener is the nail. Most often used in framing are the 16d and 8d sinker. The *d* stands for penny-weight, or penny, once the standard for weighing nails (a 16d nail would weigh the same as sixteen pennies). Sinkers are a type of nail with a vinyl coating that makes them easier to drive. For nailing any material that will be exposed to the elements, even if it is to be painted, use galvanized nails.

Figure 1 illustrates two ways of driving nails. Face nailing refers to a nail being driven through the face of one board and into another board. Toe nailing means that a nail is driven at an angle, usually through the end of one board and into another.

Deck screws are popular today and for some applications are more practical than

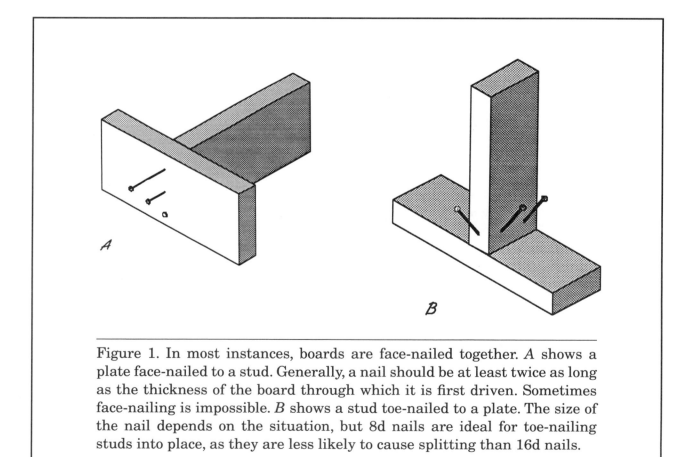

Figure 1. In most instances, boards are face-nailed together. *A* shows a plate face-nailed to a stud. Generally, a nail should be at least twice as long as the thickness of the board through which it is first driven. Sometimes face-nailing is impossible. *B* shows a stud toe-nailed to a plate. The size of the nail depends on the situation, but 8d nails are ideal for toe-nailing studs into place, as they are less likely to cause splitting than 16d nails.

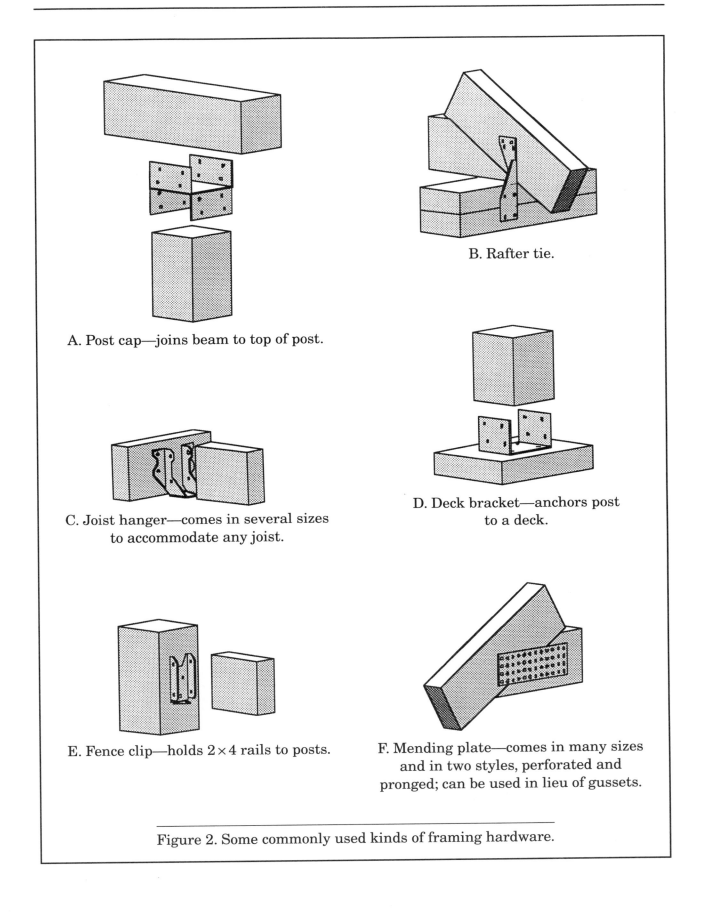

A. Post cap—joins beam to top of post.

B. Rafter tie.

C. Joist hanger—comes in several sizes
to accommodate any joist.

D. Deck bracket—anchors post
to a deck.

E. Fence clip—holds 2 × 4 rails to posts.

F. Mending plate—comes in many sizes
and in two styles, perforated and
pronged; can be used in lieu of gussets.

Figure 2. Some commonly used kinds of framing hardware.

nails, because they won't work themselves out of the wood as nails often will. As their name implies, they are excellent for decks. They are also preferable in the construction of ladders and other components exposed to constant use or stress.

Many hardware manufacturers have developed full lines of clips, anchors, straps, and hangers designed to make framing easier and stronger. Figure 2 shows the most common types of framing hardware.

In some cases, it is preferable to use framing hardware; in others, it's more a matter of convenience.

Even though using this hardware will add to the cost of a project, remember that safety and strength should be your foremost concern.

▪ Foundation and Floor Fundamentals ▪

Certainly the foundation requirements for a playhouse are much less than that of a residence. Yet, as in any construction project, a solid foundation is essential. The requirements for a playhouse foundation vary depending on the design and ground condition. Structures that are built well above the ground, such as the Fire Tower, dictate that the posts be firmly anchored for stability. Ground-level structures, such as the Alpine A-frame, are inherently stable. Their foundations need support only the weight of the structure itself. In some cases, however, it might be desirable to anchor even ground-level structures. Susceptibility to high wind, heavy frost, or poor soil conditions is a consideration.

The following discussion covers three methods of building a foundation: pier blocks, embedded posts, and concrete slab. The plans for ground-level structures in part 2 call for floor systems built of 2×6 joists covered with ¾-inch treated plywood. How the floor is supported is left to the discretion of the builder.

FOUNDATION VARIATIONS
Pier Blocks
Pier blocks are precast, trapezoidal concrete blocks that come in three configurations, as shown in Figure 3. The standard block has a hole bored through its center to receive a spike or rod driven into the bottom of a post, which will prevent lateral (side-to-side) movement of the post. The notched block is designed to receive a 2×4 or wider joist or stringer on edge or a 4×4 post on end. The bracketed block has a steel post anchor cast into it. This will receive a 4×4 post on end or a 4×4 or wider beam on edge.

Pier blocks provide instant support, but there are drawbacks. First, the standard and notched blocks provide no means of anchoring the structure. Second, if any of the blocks are exposed, a child can trip or fall on them. All three can be buried to eliminate the safety hazard, and the anchoring power of the bracketed block is increased when buried. Burying a pier block, however, defeats its purpose of keeping a post or stringer above ground level.

Embedded Post
Posts embedded in earth, gravel, or concrete are recommended for the above-ground projects, with concrete being the preferred method. Figure 4 shows a post embedded in concrete. Sacks of dry, premixed concrete products are readily available at any builders' outlet. For the taller structures, posts should be 24 to 36 inches deep. For other applications, where the posts merely support a deck close to the ground, embed them about 12 inches deep.

Before pouring any concrete, securely brace the posts so that they are plumb,

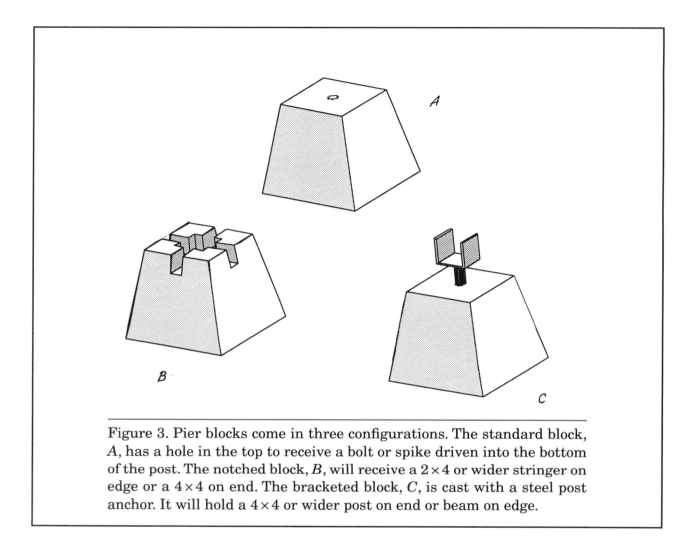

Figure 3. Pier blocks come in three configurations. The standard block, *A*, has a hole in the top to receive a bolt or spike driven into the bottom of the post. The notched block, *B*, will receive a 2×4 or wider stringer on edge or a 4×4 on end. The bracketed block, *C*, is cast with a steel post anchor. It will hold a 4×4 or wider post on end or beam on edge.

square, and correctly located. Allow at least twenty-four hours for the concrete to cure before removing the braces.

Concrete Slab

Forming a simple concrete pad is a challenge that can be met by the do-it-yourselfer, but unless you are sure of your skills, hiring a concrete mason is recommended for the actual pouring and finishing. Figure 5 shows the necessary details. The slab should be formed on relatively level ground. It's possible to form a pad on just about any terrain, but the difficulty, expense, and necessary expertise increase dramatically.

Mixing concrete by hand is arduous work, but many rental companies carry mixers and even sell ready-mixed concrete products.

BUILDING FLOORS
Where to Put the Structure

Having decided to build one of the structures in this book, you may already have a good idea of where you want to put it. The configuration of your yard may dictate placement, orientation, and even the design itself. But if you have the flexibility, consider local weather patterns before you begin building. If possible, keep playhouse door and window openings out of the path of prevailing winds and rain. Also consider how the sun will

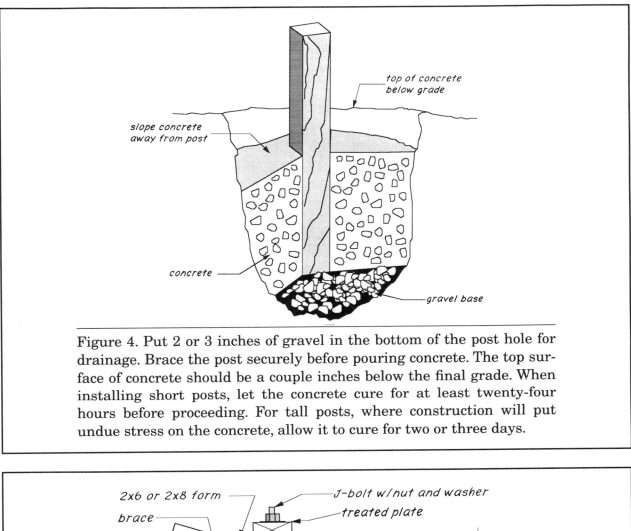

Figure 4. Put 2 or 3 inches of gravel in the bottom of the post hole for drainage. Brace the post securely before pouring concrete. The top surface of concrete should be a couple inches below the final grade. When installing short posts, let the concrete cure for at least twenty-four hours before proceeding. For tall posts, where construction will put undue stress on the concrete, allow it to cure for two or three days.

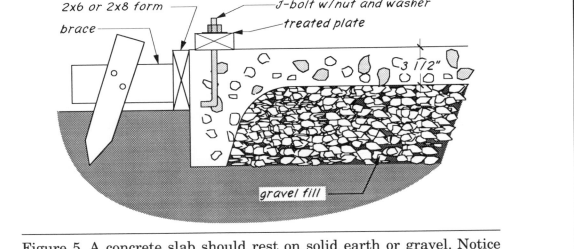

Figure 5. A concrete slab should rest on solid earth or gravel. Notice that the edges are thicker and extend below grade level. Before the concrete sets up, install a J-bolt 12 to 16 inches in from each corner, in the center of each side, and near door openings. Use pressure-treated lumber for plates.

shine on a playhouse. Will it be cool and dreary inside or bright and inviting? On the other hand, you may not want it in such direct sunlight that it could turn ovenlike on a hot summer day.

Square with the World

A well-built foundation must be square and level. By square I am referring not to the shape, but to the corners. When each of the four corners forms a 90-degree angle, the deck is square. To determine whether the foundation (or any other four-sided object) is square, measure across the diagonals. The actual length is not important. Shift the corners until both diagonal measurements are the same. When they are, the unit is square (Figure 6).

Another way to check for square is by the 3–4–5 rule (Figure 7). Measure along one side 3 feet from one corner, and mark that point. Measure 4 feet from the same corner along the adjacent side, and mark that point. Now measure the distance between the two points. When the distance is exactly 5 feet, the corner is square. You may have noticed that this is the Pythagorean theorem in disguise. The Pythagorean theorem states that $A^2+B^2=C^2$, or the sum of the squares of the lengths of the sides of a right triangle is equal to the square of the length of the hypotenuse.

Each of these methods for checking for square assumes that opposing sides are of equal length and the plane on which the corners lie is level. Otherwise you will introduce distortion.

Batter Boards

Using batter boards is a tried-and-true method of establishing level and square corners before doing any actual building. Even though you are working with a small floor area (which will make squaring the floor relatively easy without batter boards), batter boards will greatly ease the process if the ground has a lot of slope to it or if you are setting tall posts in concrete.

To set batter boards, as shown in Figure 8, first roughly locate the structure's corners with 1×2 stakes.

Next, drive three 2×4 stakes, establishing corners about 2 feet farther out from the actual corners. The stakes should extend at least 6 inches above the desired elevation of the floor.

Determine the elevation by locating the highest corner. From there, calculate how

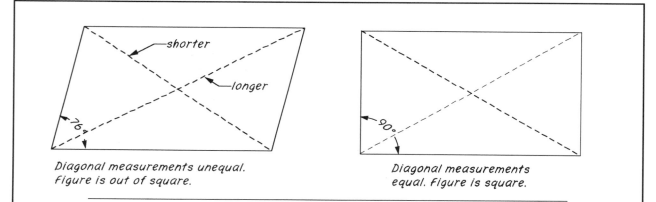

Diagonal measurements unequal. Figure is out of square.

Diagonal measurements equal. Figure is square.

Figure 6. When the diagonals are equal, the unit is square. This method of squaring an object will work only when opposing sides are of equal length.

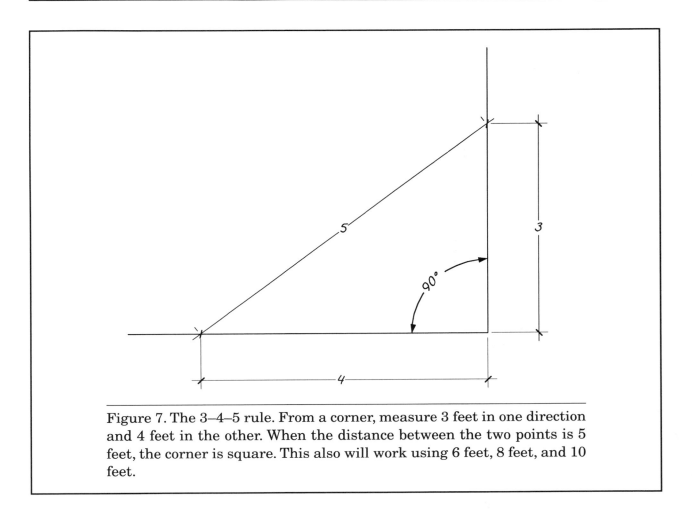

Figure 7. The 3–4–5 rule. From a corner, measure 3 feet in one direction and 4 feet in the other. When the distance between the two points is 5 feet, the corner is square. This also will work using 6 feet, 8 feet, and 10 feet.

much space you will need to incorporate the framing members, including necessary clearances. Mark this point on the corner stake. This will be the string height. Transfer the string height to the other stakes with a level and a long straightedge, a line level, or a water level. (Water levels are readily available and easy to use.) When setting batter boards for taller posts (for the Fire Tower, for example), make the stakes as high as practicable.

Nail the batter boards to the stakes at the level marks.

To establish the first side, stretch a length of builders' string across a pair of batter boards roughly above two of the small corner stakes. Tie each end to a nail driven into the outside of each board. Use two nails

in the top of the board to make a V as shown to keep the string in place.

To establish the opposite side, take the intended dimension from the plan and measure this distance from each end of the first string where it rests on the batter boards. Mark the points on the opposite boards. Secure a second string across these points.

Check the distance between the strings at each end. They must be equal. Consider these two strings as "fixed"—that is, you will not have to move them during the squaring process.

Now stretch a third string perpendicular to the first two and roughly above your 1 × 2 corner stakes. Visually determine that the string is at right angles with the first two and secure it to the batter boards.

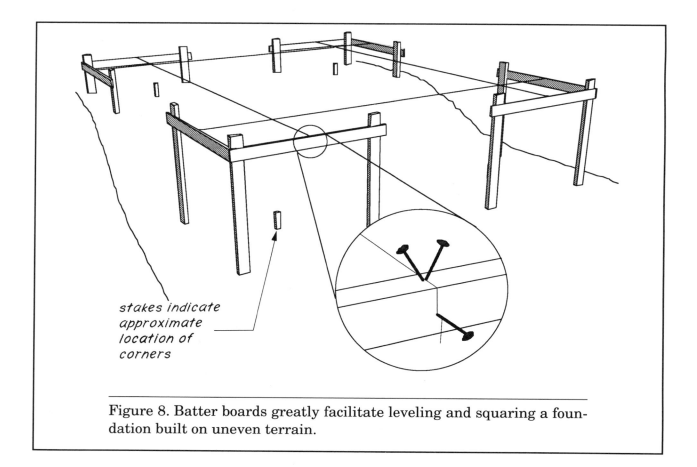

stakes indicate
approximate
location of
corners

Figure 8. Batter boards greatly facilitate leveling and squaring a foundation built on uneven terrain.

Using the adjacent dimension from the plans, measure this distance from string three at each end and secure the fourth string. You have now established a tentative perimeter of the building.

Next, measure the diagonals to check for square. When measuring diagonals and other long distances, "cut a foot" on the tape measure. That is, instead of trying to hold the end of the tape on the mark, hold the 1-foot mark at the point from which you are measuring. This allows you to get a firm grip on the tape while holding it steady on the mark. When using this method to measure actual distances, be sure to make the arithmetic adjustment.

Unless you're lucky, the diagonals won't be the same on the first try. If not, move the second set of strings right or left, in equal increments, until the diagonals are the

same. Always recheck the distances between the strings before checking the diagonals.

Once the strings are square, clear away any sod and loose dirt for pier blocks or dig holes at each corner deep enough to receive posts. Pier blocks should rest on solid, undisturbed soil. Level the blocks and locate them beneath the corners. If you have trouble reaching undisturbed soil, you may have to pour a pad of concrete on which to set the pier blocks. The pad should be about 18 inches square and 8 inches thick.

Taking care in leveling your batter boards will give you accurate points from which to measure post lengths later. As long as the string is level, the top of the posts can be at any point above, below, or on the string.

When setting strings according to the dimensions given on the plans, be sure to take into account the relationship between the posts and the stringers. For instance, if the floor is 96 inches square, and the stringers are to be secured to the outside faces of the posts, the posts will be 93 inches apart.

Set the corner posts and brace them securely. Then nail on the stringers and end joists. To complete the floor frame, follow the layout procedure outlined below. Finally, install any intermediate posts. If your floor is more than 18 inches above the ground, install braces, as shown in Figure 10.

Installing Floor without Batter Boards

Again, the use of batter boards will facilitate construction when you are working on a hillside or setting tall posts. When building a small floor on reasonably level ground, it's much easier to frame the floor first and then secure it to posts or pier blocks. It's a bit like putting the cart before the horse, but it works.

Choose a firm, level area, such as a garage floor, on which to work. Cut all the joists and stringers to length. Then nail the stringers and end joists together with three 16d galvanized nails to form the perimeter frame.

Next, lay out the joists 24 inches on center (OC). To do so, hook your tape measure at one corner and mark the stringer at 23¼ inches. Make an x to the right of this mark (Figure 9). Place the end of your tape measure on the first mark, and mark off 24 inch increments until you reach the end of the stringer. Repeat the process on the opposite side. Using a combination square, draw lines on the inside faces of the stringers to which you will nail the joists. The xs indicate on which side of the line the joists are nailed. Notice the importance of placing the fist mark at 23¼ inches from the end.

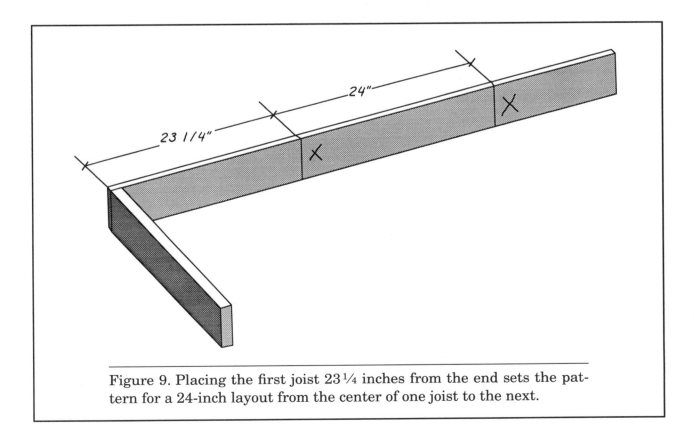

Figure 9. Placing the first joist 23¼ inches from the end sets the pattern for a 24-inch layout from the center of one joist to the next.

Doing so establishes an on-center pattern, which means that it is 24 inches from the outside of the first joist to the center of the next, and so on. Nail the joists in place using three 16d galvanized nails at each end. Alternatively, you can use 2×6 joist hangers.

Solid bridging, the short blocks between the joists in Figure 10, helps to distribute a concentrated load among all the joists. Ideally, bridging should run through the center of the span. In some cases, however, it can serve as backing for the joint between two pieces of plywood flooring. If such a joint occurs away from the center of the span, it may be feasible to locate the bridging under the joint.

Once the main floor frame is assembled, check it for square. When it is right, hold it in place by nailing a temporary 1×4 brace diagonally across the frame.

Carry the assembled frame to the construction site. If you are supporting the floor with pier blocks, make sure they are on solid, undisturbed soil. Level the floor as needed.

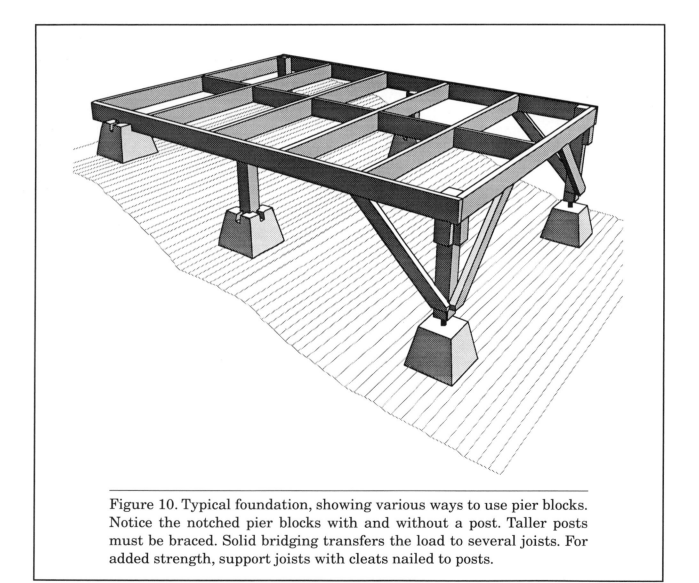

Figure 10. Typical foundation, showing various ways to use pier blocks. Notice the notched pier blocks with and without a post. Taller posts must be braced. Solid bridging transfers the load to several joists. For added strength, support joists with cleats nailed to posts.

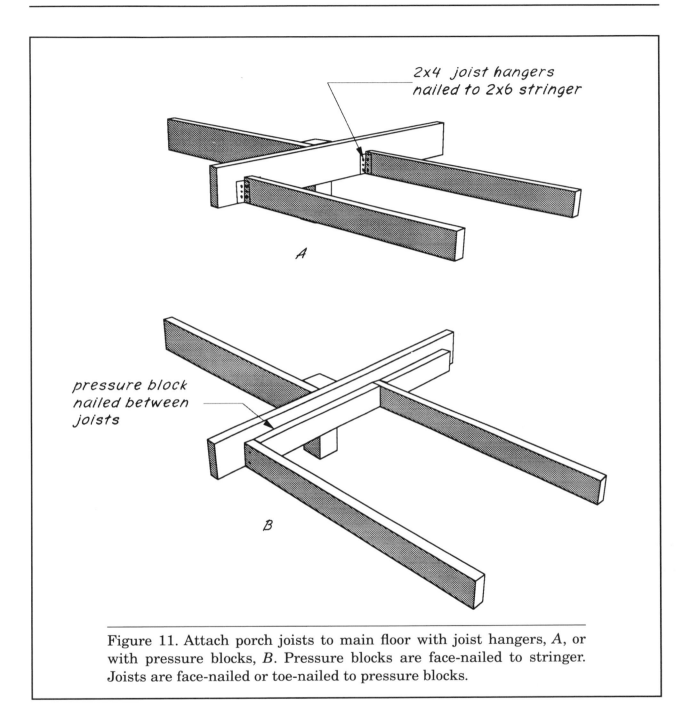

Figure 11. Attach porch joists to main floor with joist hangers, *A*, or with pressure blocks, *B*. Pressure blocks are face-nailed to stringer. Joists are face-nailed or toe-nailed to pressure blocks.

If you plan to use embedded posts, mark the positions of the holes, move the frame aside, then dig the holes. Make sure the holes are wide enough so that you can get plenty of concrete or gravel around the posts. Reposition the frame and use blocks of wood to level it. Now it's a simple matter to measure the posts and nail them in place. Pour concrete or gravel around the posts.

After the concrete has set, secure the flooring with 8d galvanized nails.

Figure 11 shows two methods of attaching the front porch to the main floor. You can use joist hangers or angle brackets to secure the joists to the stringers, as shown in 11-A. Or you can face-nail the joists to the forwardmost stringer and nail the aftermost end to blocks nailed to the 2 × 6 stringer, as shown in 11-B. Alternatively, you can build a frame, similar to the main floor, and nail it in place later.

If your porch has short posts (such as shown on the cover) they should be embedded in the ground to help resist lateral movement.

The decking material will need to be notched around the porch posts. If necessary, nail small blocks of wood to the posts to support the decking at the notches.

▪ Framing Fundamentals ▪

BUILDING WALLS

The following description of wall framing is based on the double-wall construction method, as shown in Figure 12. In this technique, ¹⁄₂-inch plywood or OSB is nailed to the outside of the studs. Siding is then applied over the sheathing (although nailed to the studs), hence the double wall. The advantage of double-wall construction is its superior bracing capabilities. All walls must be braced to maintain rigidity and to resist shearing strain. There are other ways to brace a wall—with a let-in brace or steel strap, for example—but sheathing does the best job overall. Although siding such as T-1-11 performs this function by itself, not all siding does; therefore, sheathing is specified.

Adding sheathing increases the wall thickness to 4 inches. Perimeter dimensions given in the project plans *include* sheathing, which when installed is flush with the outside edge of the floor, unless otherwise noted. If you choose not to use sheathing, or to use sheathing but with the face of the studs flush with the edge of the floor, remember to make the necessary adjustments. You may also have to recalculate rafter lengths.

There are two kinds of walls: load bearing and non-load bearing. A bearing wall is one that supports a load other than its own, usually a roof. A nonbearing wall is one that carries no appreciable load. General practice is to space studs at 16 inches on center, as explained under "Lay Out the Plates." In most cases it may be practical, as well as cost effective, to space the studs at 24 inches on center without a sacrifice in structural integrity.

Cut the Plates

An efficient way to lay out walls is to do them all at once. Doing so allows you to get an exact count of studs and other framing members so that you can cut them all at once. Snap lines 4 inches in from the perimeter of the floor. The lines represent the inside of the wall.

Figure 13 shows a typical plate layout. The side walls run from end to end of the deck, and the end walls stand between them. (The term "side walls" refers to the walls that run from one end of the deck to the other, not necessarily what many would consider the "sides" of a house.)

Cut the top and bottom plates for the side walls to length. Tack each of the bottom plates to the deck with an 8d nail at each end. Then tack the matching top plates directly on top of the bottom plates.

The distance between these two sets of plates is the length of the end walls. Cut the end-wall plates and tack them into place.

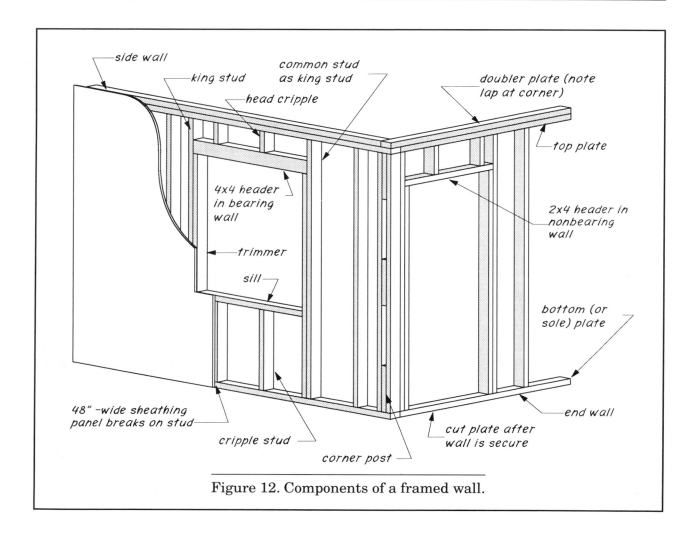

Figure 12. Components of a framed wall.

Do not cut the bottom plate where a door opening occurs. You will cut this away once the wall is up and secured.

Lay Out the Plates

Start your layout at the left end of one of the side walls. The layout procedure for walls is the same as that described in the section on floors, but the common studs are ordinarily placed at 16-inch intervals. Measure 15¼ inches from the end of the top plate. From there measure off 16-inch increments until you reach the end of the plate, placing an *x* to the right of each mark. Square a line down the outside edge of each plate at each of the marks, as shown in Figure 13.

Beginning at the 15¼-inch mark, place every stud at 16 inches on center from the corner. To lay out the end walls, measure 15¼ inches from a point ½ inch *beyond* the edge of the side-wall plate. Continue from this mark at 16-inch intervals.

Now lay out the horizontal dimensions of the door and window openings.

Note: The rough openings given in the plans are arbitrary insofar as they represent a manner of balance and symmetry in the design. They are by no means mandatory. Your final treatment of the doors and windows will have a bearing on the actual dimensions of the rough openings. Rough openings are given in inches, for example, 18×36. The first figure is the horizontal dimension, and the second figure the vertical dimension. For more information, refer to the section on "Doors and Windows."

Notice in Figure 12 that two framing members—the king studs and trimmers, together in pairs—define the horizontal dimensions of the openings. A king stud is the same as a common stud except that it has a trimmer nailed to it. A common stud in its regular layout can serve as a king stud.

The length of the trimmer, which is nailed to the bottom plate and to the inside of the king stud, determines the header height and, therefore, the top of the rough opening. The header height is not the same as the length of the trimmer because the trimmer sits on the plate.

The distance between the trimmers is the width of the rough opening (which is the sill length for windows). The distance between the king studs is the length of the

header, which is 3 inches longer than the rough opening is wide.

Chances are that one or both of the king studs will be near, or overlapping, a common stud. If a common stud interferes with a king stud, eliminate it. Alternatively, you can shift the opening to the nearest common stud and use it as a king stud.

Headers and Sills. With the layout complete, measure and cut all the studs, cripples, trimmers, headers, and sills.

The function of a header, aside from forming the top of the opening, is to carry the increased load where studs have been removed to form the opening. The size of the header depends on the width of the opening and whether it is in a bearing or nonbearing wall.

Loads carried by bearing walls in the playhouses are relatively small, and a single 2×4 nailed flatways will usually be sufficient for a header, especially when the wall

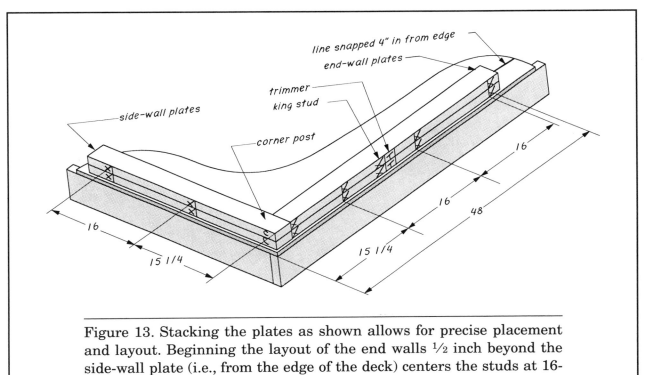

Figure 13. Stacking the plates as shown allows for precise placement and layout. Beginning the layout of the end walls ½ inch beyond the side-wall plate (i.e., from the edge of the deck) centers the studs at 16-inch intervals from the corners.

is sheathed. In most of the projects, however, a 4×4 header is indicated for openings in bearing walls. A 4×4 header can be cut from solid stock or built up from two 2×4s with a ½-inch spacer between.

A single 2×4 is sufficient for the sill.

Build the Walls

For the larger models, you will be able to build a wall right on the deck, raise it, and nail it to the floor before proceeding with the next wall. For the smaller models, it will be necessary to build a wall and set it aside before building the next one. Then you can bring the walls together in one operation.

The first step in constructing the walls is to build up the corner posts, each of which is made of two studs with three pieces of scrap 2×4 about 12 inches long nailed between them (see Figure 12). You will need four posts, one for each end of the side walls.

When building the posts, keep the ends even.

Lay the plates of the first wall on the deck with the stud marks up. The order in which you nail the components together isn't important. Use two 16d nails driven through the plate into the end of each stud. Trimmers are nailed to the bottom plate and to their king studs. Drive two nails near the top end of each trimmer, two near the bottom, and one or two up the center. Because 16d nails are 3½ inches long, they will protrude through the king stud. To prevent a cut finger, either clinch the nail or use shorter 10d nails for the purpose.

To finish the window openings, measure down from the bottom of the header the vertical dimension of the opening and mark each trimmer accordingly. Nail the sill into place below the marks, nail in the cripple studs, then nail in the rest of the studs.

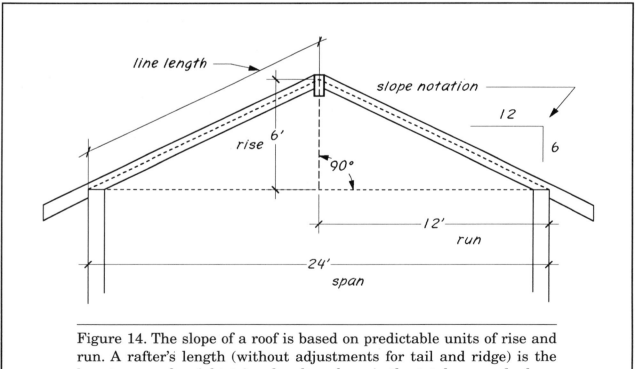

Figure 14. The slope of a roof is based on predictable units of rise and run. A rafter's length (without adjustments for tail and ridge) is the hypotenuse of a right triangle whose base is the total run and whose side is the total rise above the plate.

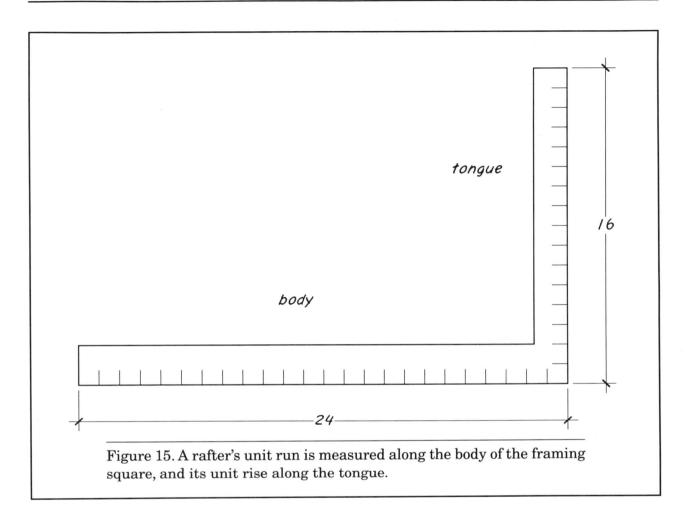

tongue

body

16

24

Figure 15. A rafter's unit run is measured along the body of the framing square, and its unit rise along the tongue.

Notice in Figure 12 how the doubler plates of the end walls overlap the top plates of the side walls. For the side walls, cut a 2×4 7 inches shorter than the length of the wall. Nail it to the top plate 3½ inches in from each end.

Sheathing can be applied to the side walls before or after they are raised. If applying it beforehand, the walls first must be squared. Place the wall on the floor or other firm, flat surface, then measure the diagonals of the wall. *Do not* include the doubler plate in your measurement. Push the top of the wall one way or the other to bring the wall into square.

Now nail down the sheathing. Do not let the wall move out of square during the process. It is easiest to nail the sheathing

right over door and window openings, then cut out the openings before lifting the wall. Transfer the measurements of the openings to the sheathing. Use a chalk line to mark the openings. Set your saw for ½ inch and cut out the waste.

Because the sheathing on the end walls runs across the ends of the side walls, you will not be able to fully sheath them until after they are raised and secured. If the wall is long enough, you can sheath the mid portion before raising, and fill in the ends with scraps later.

Lift each wall, securely bracing it in place before moving on. Nail the bottom plate to the floor, into the joists or stringers wherever possible. Nail down the overlapping doubler plates. Sight down the tops of the walls to make sure they are straight. If not, use a brace to push the top of the wall in or out where necessary.

Now you are ready to begin the roof.

BUILDING ROOFS
Rise, Run, and Span Defined

Building a roof presents perhaps the biggest challenge in framing. But once you understand a few basic terms and procedures, it is a challenge that can be met.

Figure 14 illustrates a roof's rise, run, and span. The span is the outside-to-outside distance from wall to wall. The run is

exactly half the span. The rise is how high the rafter rises over the run. The example shows a span of 24 feet, a run of 12 feet, and a rise of 6 feet.

The rise and run of any roof are further broken down into units that describe a roof's pitch, slope, or cut, based on inches. The unit run is always set at 12 inches, and the unit rise is determined by how many inches the roof rises in 12 inches of run.

The roof in Figure 14 has a 6-in-12 pitch. In other words, for every 12 inches of run, the roof rises 6 inches. The small right angle shown is the standard symbol indicating the

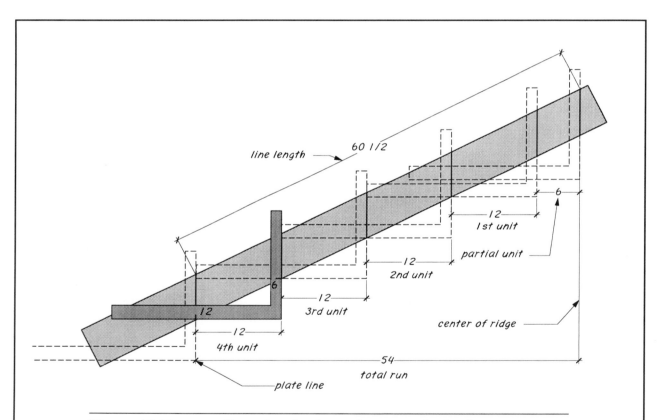

Figure 16. To step off a rafter, begin at the top with the framing square set at the desired slope, shown here as 6-in-12. Draw a plumb line along the tongue. Lay out the partial unit first, in this case 6 inches, measuring horizontally along the body of the square. Then move the square down the rafter, keeping it oriented correctly, and step off each full unit (12 inches) of run. Use a sharp pencil, and do not let the square gain as you move along the rafter.

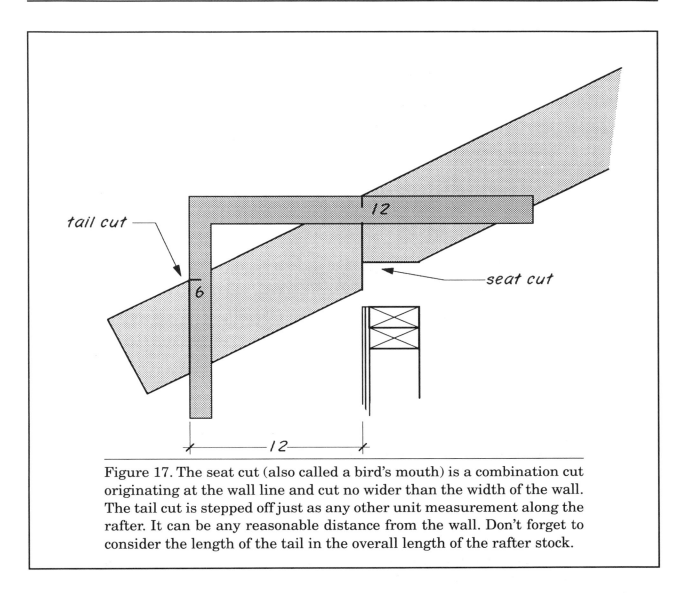

Figure 17. The seat cut (also called a bird's mouth) is a combination cut originating at the wall line and cut no wider than the width of the wall. The tail cut is stepped off just as any other unit measurement along the rafter. It can be any reasonable distance from the wall. Don't forget to consider the length of the tail in the overall length of the rafter stock.

pitch of the roof. (Technically, the pitch of a roof is presented as a fraction based on the ratio of rise to span instead of inches of rise to inches of run. A 6-in-12 roof has a pitch of $6/24$, which is further reduced to $1/4$. Conventionally, however, the terms pitch, slope, and cut are used interchangeably.)

Using the Framing Square to Lay Out Rafters

The framing square is the most useful tool for determining the length of a rafter and laying out the necessary cuts.

The square has two legs: the longer, wider body and the tongue (Figure 15). The unit run is always set by the body, and the unit rise by the tongue. Level cuts are marked along the body, and plumb cuts along the tongue.

To determine the length of a common rafter, first select a straight piece of stock to use as a pattern, and place it across a set of sawhorses. Orient yourself so that you can visualize the cut rafter as it rises in the air.

Measure the span (the outside-to-outside distance between the bearing walls). Assume for this example a span of 9 feet.

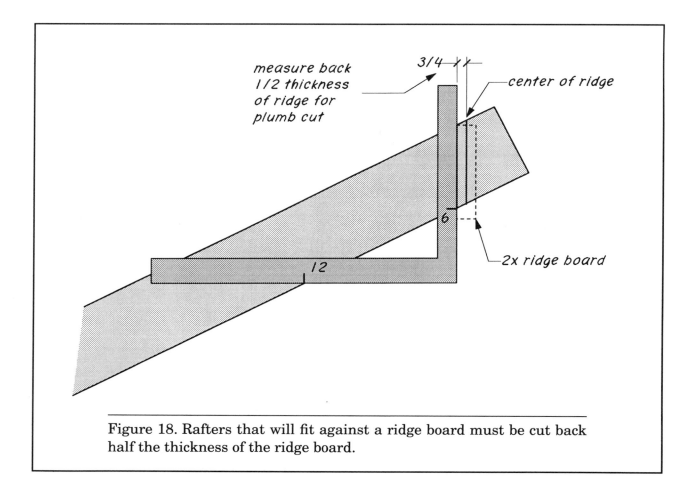

measure back
1/2 thickness
of ridge for
plumb cut

3/4

center of ridge

2x ridge board

6

12

Figure 18. Rafters that will fit against a ridge board must be cut back half the thickness of the ridge board.

The total run, then, is 4 feet 6 inches (4 ½ units). The unit rise is 6 inches.

Place the framing square as shown in Figure 16 at the top of the rafter, with the 6-inch mark on the *outside* of the tongue and the 12-inch mark on the *outside* of the body intersecting the lower edge of the stock. Be very precise about this placement, and with a sharp pencil, draw a line along the tongue. This is the upper plumb cut.

In our example we have a partial, or odd, unit of 6 inches. Lay this out first. Without moving the square from the plumb cut, measure 6 inches along the body of the square from the outside corner and mark the rafter stock at that point. Now slide the square down the rafter until the tongue is on this mark.

Consider purchasing a pair of stair

gauges or other devices to clip onto the square at the desired points. These will allow you to readily place the square in the correct orientation each time you move it. A pair of small C clamps will work in a pinch.

With the square properly placed at the odd unit, put a mark at 12 inches, where the body of the square intersects with the lower edge of the rafter. This is the first full unit. Repeat this step three more times. Draw a plumb cut at the bottom end of the fourth unit. The distance between the top and bottom plumb cuts is the rafter's line length (less the tail). In this case, the length is 4 feet, 10 ½ inches.

Now lay out the tail and seat cuts, as shown in Figure 17. If the overhang is to be 12 inches, simply step off one more full unit and mark the plumb cut. If the fascia board will be included in the overhang, measure back the thickness of the fascia. Working this close to the end of the rafter stock, you may need to flip the square. Cut the rafter at both plumb cuts to use as a pattern for your barge rafters.

Select four of your best pieces of rafter stock for the barge rafters, cut them, and set them aside.

If the remaining rafters are to fit against a ridge board (i.e., they are not going to be used for trusses, explained later), you must shorten the pattern by half the thickness of the ridge board. Measure this distance horizontally, as shown in Figure 18.

Recut the pattern at the ridge and make the seat cut. When cutting the seat, you can use a circular saw, but do not go past the inside corner on either the level or the plumb cuts. Finish the cuts with a hand saw. You are now ready to use the pattern to mark, then cut, the rest of the rafters.

Before raising the rafters, lay out, cut, and install the ceiling joists. Ceiling joists support the ceiling material, if any, and tie the bearing walls together. Without them, the load on the rafters could force the peak down and the walls apart.

Lay out the joists 24 inches on center along both plates of the bearing walls. The

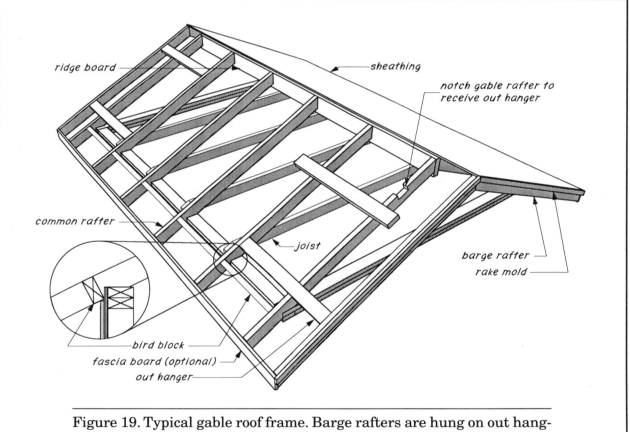

Figure 19. Typical gable roof frame. Barge rafters are hung on out hangers notched into gable rafters and nailed to the first common rafters. Rake mold conceals sheathing edges. Bird blocks give a straight edge against which to abut siding. For enclosed attics, bore four or five 1-inch-diameter holes into each block, and back with screen for ventilation.

joists will go on the right side of the line, the rafters on the left. The length of the joists will be the same as the span, or a little less. Notice in Figure 19 that you will have to nip the top corner of the joists to conform to the slope of the roof.

Raising the Roof. The rafters are nailed to a ridge board at the peak. Barge rafters, also called fly rafters, form the overhang on the gable ends of the roof and are supported by out hangers, or lookouts, as shown in Figure 19. An optional fascia board covers the rafter tails. For overhangs of 6 inches or less, the sheathing itself will support the barge rafters, provided that the sheathing extends into the body of the roof.

Lay out the ridge board to correspond with the layout on the plate, making sure that you locate the rafters on the correct side of the line.

One or two assistants will be of help in raising the rafters. With the ridge elevated, pull up a pair of rafters at one end and nail them first to the ridge, then to the plate. Do the same at the other end. Brace the ridge and nail in the rest of the common rafters, including the gable and barge rafters, and the fascia boards.

Bird blocks fit between the rafters, closing the space between the wall and the roof. They also form a straight line against which to abut the siding at the top of the wall. Alternatively, you can notch the siding around the rafters and run it up to the roof sheathing. If you plan to cover the inside walls and ceiling, bore 1-inch holes in the bird blocks and cover with screen for attic ventilation.

Frame in the gable studs (Figure 20), beginning with the one directly under the ridge. Make sure the gables are plumb and the ridge is straight before nailing on the

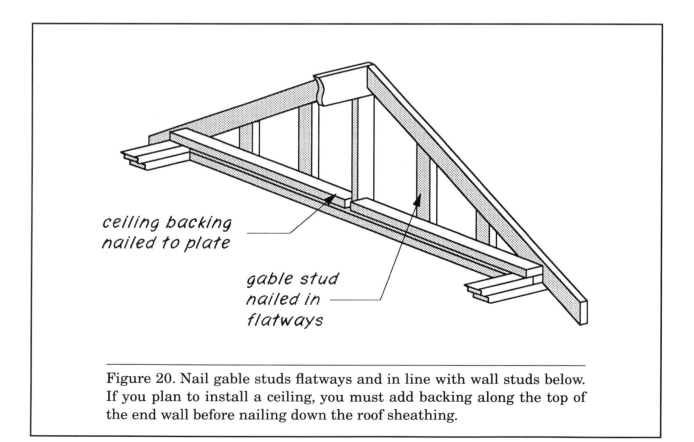

ceiling backing nailed to plate

gable stud nailed in flatways

Figure 20. Nail gable studs flatways and in line with wall studs below. If you plan to install a ceiling, you must add backing along the top of the end wall before nailing down the roof sheathing.

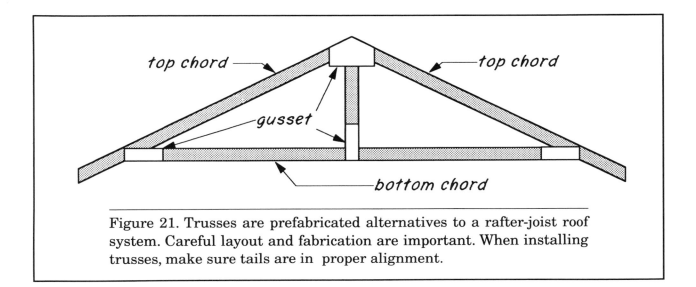

Figure 21. Trusses are prefabricated alternatives to a rafter-joist roof system. Careful layout and fabrication are important. When installing trusses, make sure tails are in proper alignment.

sheathing. Nail the sheathing every 6 inches along the edges and 12 inches in the field or interior portion of the sheathing.

Use rake molding to cover the edges of the sheathing on the gable ends, as shown in Figure 19. A good choice for rake molding is 1×2 cedar.

Trusses

Roof trusses are a simple alternative to a stick-framed roof. A truss, Figure 21, is a single, structurally sound prefabricated unit. The individual members are held together with plywood gussets glued and nailed or with commercially available steel nailing plates. The pieces that form the perimeter of the truss—those that corre-spond to the rafters and joists—are called chords.

Care must be taken that all trusses are exactly the same and are aligned correctly along the tops of the walls. Lay out each piece on a large, flat surface. Apply gussets to one side, then flip the truss for the gussets on the other side. Do not use plywood gussets on the outside of the gable trusses, as they will interfere with sheathing or siding.

No ridge board is used on a trussed roof. Trusses are nailed to the plate as rafters are, and they are temporarily held in alignment at the peak with a 1×4 until enough sheathing is nailed down to do the job. Be sure the gables are plumb before nailing on the sheathing.

▪ Dressing Up ▪

First you decided to build a playhouse. Then you decided which one. Now it's up and ready to accommodate a neighborhood of kids. You may consider it to be finished at this point, but on the other hand, you may feel as though you're not even halfway there.

Truly, there is no limit to the possibilities for enhancing a playhouse, from the practical, such as roofing and screened windows, to the fanciful, such as gingerbread trim and a neo-Victorian "painted lady" look.

ROOFING

No doubt you've heard the old story about the guy who complained of a leaky roof. When a neighbor suggested he fix it, the man indignantly replied that he couldn't be expected to climb up on the roof in the pouring rain. The next day, when the sun came out, the neighbor suggested that his friend take advantage of the good weather and fix the roof. "What for?" said the man. "It's not leaking."

A leaky roof on a playhouse certainly won't cause the same degree of problems it would on your home. But it will decrease the longevity of the playhouse and prohibit use during rainy weather. Of course, if you live in a climate that has little rainfall, the condition of the roof may not matter much.

A variety of roofing materials are available, ranging in style and ease of application as much as they do in price. Yet because your playhouse is relatively small, even for a more expensive type of roof the cost is also relatively small.

Roofs and roofing materials are measured in units called squares. A square covers 100 square feet. Shingles, whether composition or wood, are further broken down into bundles. How many bundles make up a square depends on the weight, size, and composition of the material.

There are too many different kinds of roofing materials to allow for practical discussion here. Some guidelines, based on residential construction practices, will be helpful, however. For pitches less than 4-in-12, roll roofing (Figure 22) is recommended. For pitches of 4-in-12 or greater, three-tab composition shingles (Figure 23) are recommended. Wood shingles (Figure 24) are an attractive alternative to composition shingles for roofs 5-in-12 or greater. Wood shingles also can be used as siding.

For more information about roofing materials and how to install them, see your building materials supplier.

DOORS AND WINDOWS

Simple door and window openings are all that are necessary for your playhouse, but you may wish to keep the elements out. A cross-buck door and window shutters made of ¾-inch plywood and 1 × 4s will do nicely for this purpose.

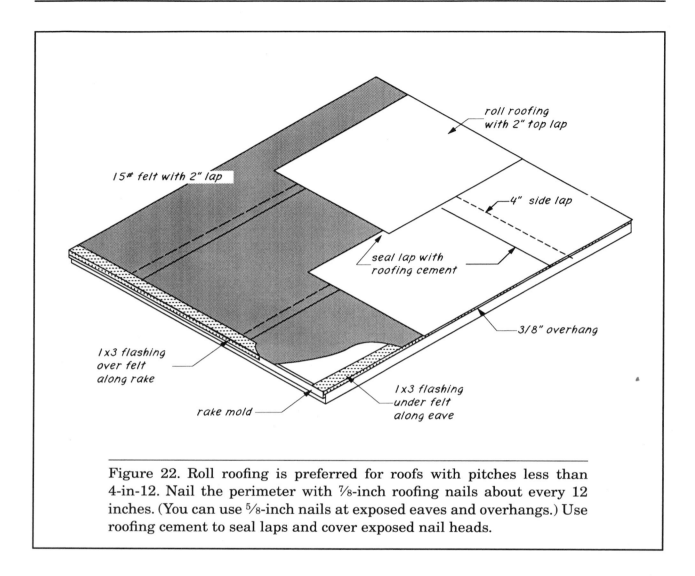

roll roofing
with 2" top lap

15# felt with 2" lap

4" side lap

seal lap with
roofing cement

3/8" overhang

1x3 flashing
over felt
along rake

1x3 flashing
under felt
along eave

rake mold

Figure 22. Roll roofing is preferred for roofs with pitches less than 4-in-12. Nail the perimeter with ⅞-inch roofing nails about every 12 inches. (You can use ⅝-inch nails at exposed eaves and overhangs.) Use roofing cement to seal laps and cover exposed nail heads.

Figure 25 shows how to make single and double shutters. Figure 26 illustrates a standard and a Dutch door.

If you'd like to take your playhouse further into the land of authenticity, you may prefer glazed windows and solid-core doors that are fully weather-tight.

Safety note: The Uniform Building Code states that glass coming within 18 inches of a floor, within 12 inches of a door, or within a door itself must be tempered. For reasons of safety, however, I strongly recommend that *no glass be used* in your playhouse. Instead, glaze your windows with acrylic plastic.

Your building materials supplier may have on hand, or may be able to order, stock windows that will fit the rough openings specified in the plans. The smaller-than-standard doors, however, will require custom fitting.

Many cities and towns have outlets for recycled building materials. Used windows can be refinished, and quite often used doors can be cut down to fit specific needs.

If you plan to buy windows and doors, do so *before* you begin construction so that you can determine the correct rough openings to suit your needs. The rough openings given in the plans are not absolute. If you have any questions about specific rough openings, see your supplier.

SIDING, TRIM, AND PAINTING

The exterior finishing touches on your playhouse are the siding, trim, and paint job.

Like roofing, siding serves the dual purposes of protecting the structure from the elements and enhancing its overall beauty. Also like roofing, there are many styles and methods of application of siding. For playhouses, however, some are more practical than others.

Plywood siding, T-1-11, is applied verti-

cally. It comes in 3/8- and 5/8-inch thickness. The thicker panels come with a variety of vertical groove patterns to simulate individual boards. The 3/8-inch panels have no grooves. You can dress up 3/8-inch T-1-11 with 1×2 battens nailed to the studs (Figure 27). Corner boards and other trim are nailed atop the siding.

Although T-1-11 comes in 8-, 9-, and 10-foot lengths, the 8-foot length is most common. Unless you can acquire longer lengths, special considerations must be made on gable ends where the siding may not reach the peak within the length of one sheet.

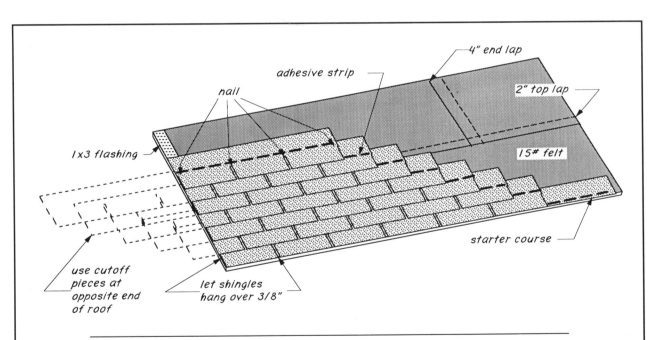

Figure 23. Three-tab composition shingles come in a variety of styles and weights and are easy to apply. The self-sealing asphalt strip is activated by heat from the sun and securely holds the tabs of the shingles in the succeeding course. For the starter course, remove the tabs from sufficient shingles to cover the length of the eave. Cut 6 inches from the left end of the first length of the starter course and nail to the roof through the adhesive strip. Use a full shingle to begin the first course, nailing it directly over the starter strip. Cut 6 inches from the left end of the first shingle in the second course, 12 inches from the left end of the second course, and so on as shown. Use cutoff pieces at the opposite end of the roof.

Making a horizontal splice presents a problem of water infiltration. There are two common methods to counteract leakage, as illustrated in Figure 28. The first, *A*, makes use of a piece of flashing designed for the purpose. The break in the siding should occur over solid backing.

The second method, *B*, makes use of an overlap caused by moving the gable rafter and studs out far enough to create the necessary offset. This is also an excellent method if you want to combine two different kinds of siding, for example, horizontal on the body of the playhouse and shingles or plywood on the gables.

There are many different kinds of horizontal siding materials made of wood or wood products, such as Masonite. Figure 29 shows a typical installation of bevel siding. Generally, corner boards and other trim should go on before horizontal siding.

Always follow the manufacturer's instructions when installing siding. This is especially important when installing Masonite siding, as it expands and contracts much more than wood with changes in humidity.

Just as on your home, a good paint job will protect your playhouse from the weather. Use a quality paint or stain. Latex-based products are easy to use and clean up and offer excellent protection when applied properly. At least two coats of paint or stain are necessary. Many painters use a less-expensive primer for the base coat, then apply two coats of paint over this. If you

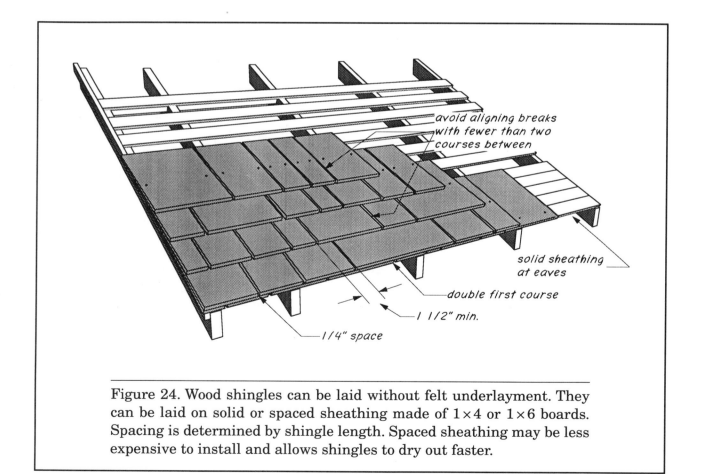

Figure 24. Wood shingles can be laid without felt underlayment. They can be laid on solid or spaced sheathing made of 1×4 or 1×6 boards. Spacing is determined by shingle length. Spaced sheathing may be less expensive to install and allows shingles to dry out faster.

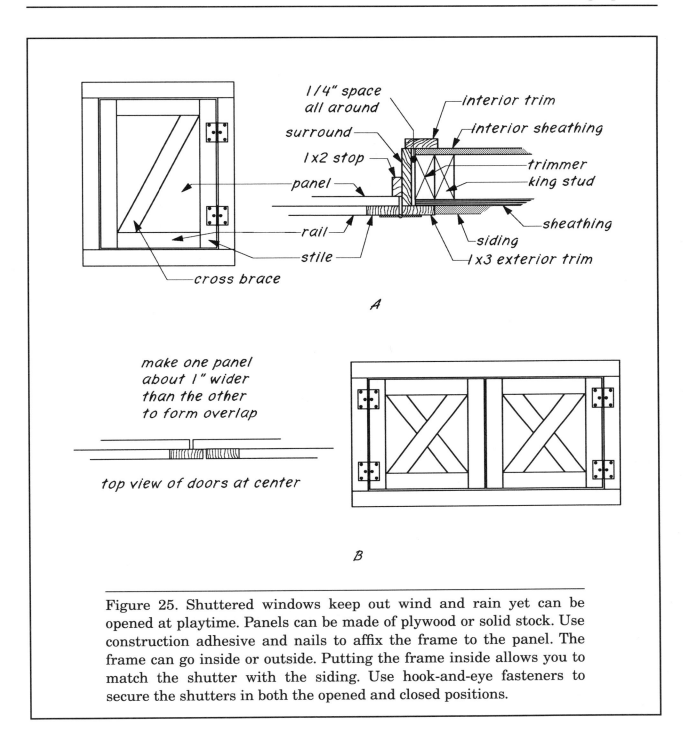

Figure 25. Shuttered windows keep out wind and rain yet can be opened at playtime. Panels can be made of plywood or solid stock. Use construction adhesive and nails to affix the frame to the panel. The frame can go inside or outside. Putting the frame inside allows you to match the shutter with the siding. Use hook-and-eye fasteners to secure the shutters in both the opened and closed positions.

have the space, consider priming and applying the first color coat to your materials before installing them. This is especially good for areas that will be hard to reach later, under the eaves, for example, and for exposed decking material whose sides will be concealed but would benefit from the added protection.

INTERIORS
The interior of your playhouse can be left unfinished, but, depending on the model,

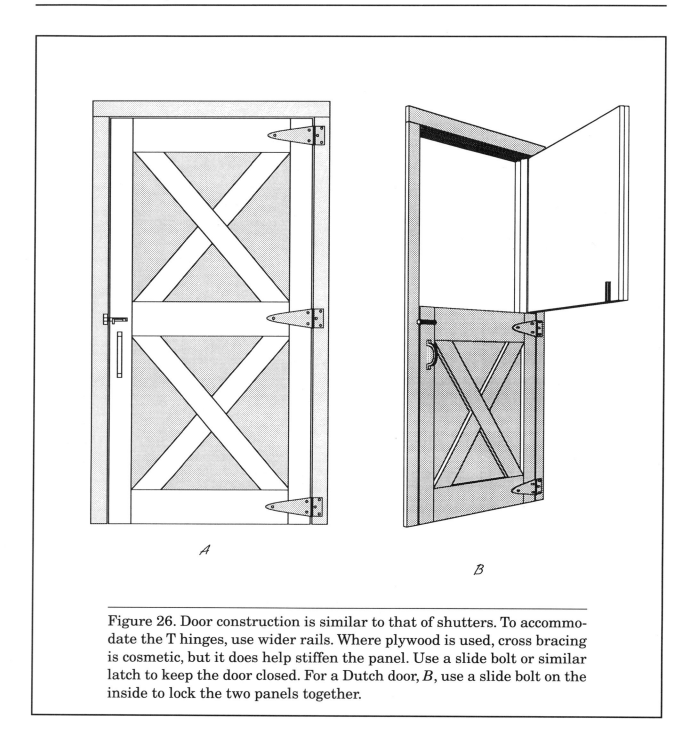

Figure 26. Door construction is similar to that of shutters. To accommodate the T hinges, use wider rails. Where plywood is used, cross bracing is cosmetic, but it does help stiffen the panel. Use a slide bolt or similar latch to keep the door closed. For a Dutch door, *B*, use a slide bolt on the inside to lock the two panels together.

you may wish to make some enhancements. Following are a few suggestions.

If there are nails poking through the sheathing where children could get hurt on them, some kind of wall covering is called for. Use 3/8- or 1/2-inch CCX plywood or OSB.

Either will take paint nicely. You can install paneling over the plywood.

Cover the ceiling with gypsum board, plywood, or OSB. Gypsum board (Sheetrock) is not recommended unless the playhouse is weather-tight.

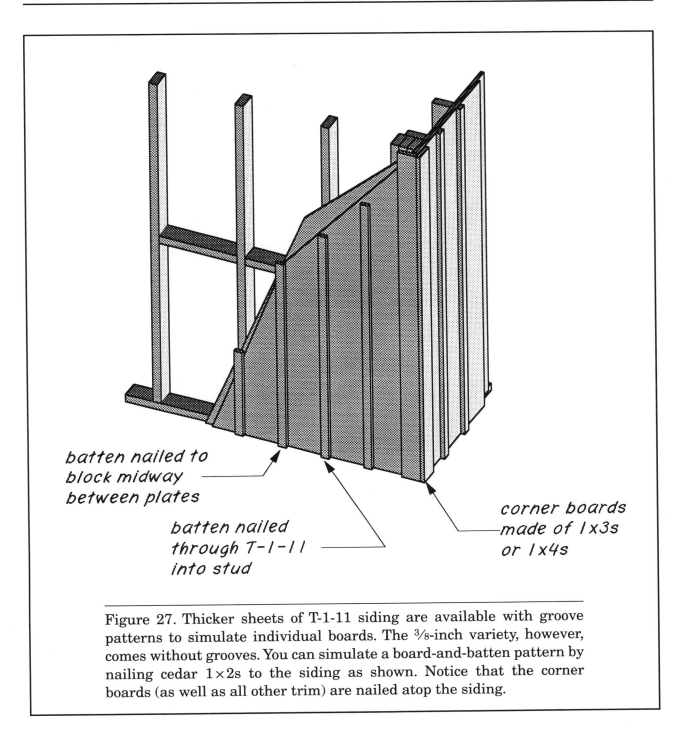

batten nailed to
block midway
between plates

batten nailed
through T-1-11
into stud

corner boards
made of 1x3s
or 1x4s

Figure 27. Thicker sheets of T-1-11 siding are available with groove patterns to simulate individual boards. The $\frac{3}{8}$-inch variety, however, comes without grooves. You can simulate a board-and-batten pattern by nailing cedar 1×2s to the siding as shown. Notice that the corner boards (as well as all other trim) are nailed atop the siding.

Painting the walls a light color not only will brighten the interior, but also will make the playhouse feel bigger.

Put two or three coats of deck enamel on the floor, or lay indoor-outdoor carpeting.

You can brighten the interior of the playhouse with a recessed ceiling light, and even install one or two wall outlets. Consult with a certified electrician before covering the walls.

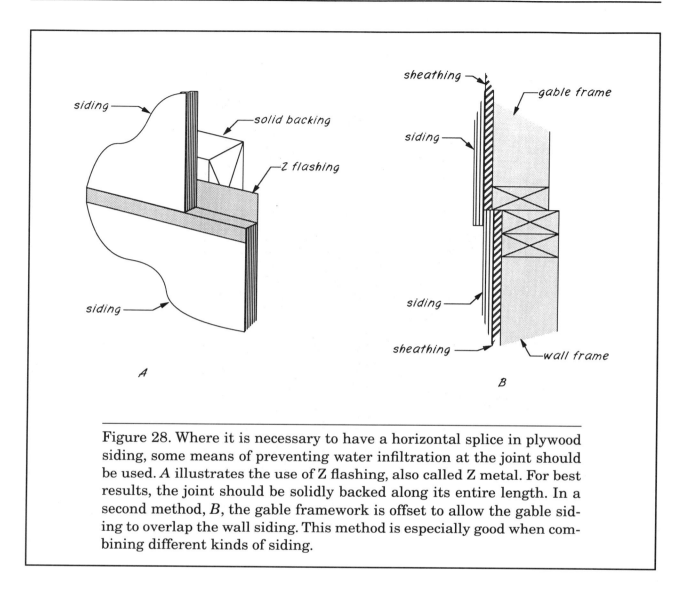

Figure 28. Where it is necessary to have a horizontal splice in plywood siding, some means of preventing water infiltration at the joint should be used. *A* illustrates the use of Z flashing, also called Z metal. For best results, the joint should be solidly backed along its entire length. In a second method, *B*, the gable framework is offset to allow the gable siding to overlap the wall siding. This method is especially good when combining different kinds of siding.

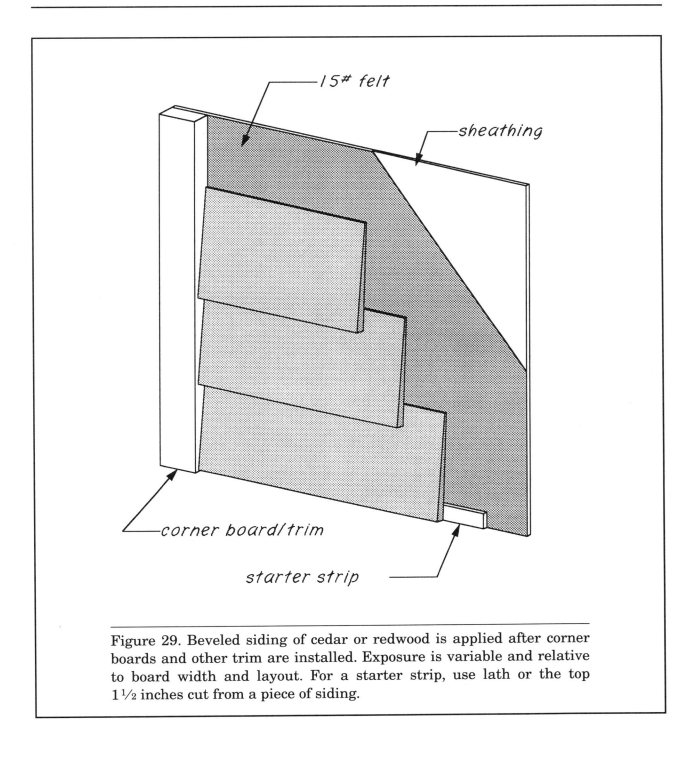

Figure 29. Beveled siding of cedar or redwood is applied after corner boards and other trim are installed. Exposure is variable and relative to board width and layout. For a starter strip, use lath or the top 1½ inches cut from a piece of siding.

■ PART II ■

The Projects

The material list that accompanies each project includes only those materials needed to frame that particular project. Roofing, siding, doors, windows, trim, and interior finish materials are at the builder's discretion, and it is up to the builder to determine what is necessary. Framing lumber comes in lengths of 2-foot increments, generally beginning at 8 feet. Many of the framing members—studs, for example—are less than 6 feet, so it is cost effective to order 12-foot 2 × 4s and get two studs out of each.

Posts to support the main floor are figured at 24 inches long unless otherwise noted. Lengths of other posts are generally listed at 24 inches longer than the above-ground dimensions shown in the plans. *Note:* These lengths assume a level grade. The builder is advised to take slope and other ground conditions into consideration when ordering posts.

Another variable is pier blocks. Materials lists specify a recommended number of piers but make no reference to a particular kind. It is up to the builder to determine specific needs regarding piers. Materials lists do not include concrete mix unless posts embedded in concrete are necessary for the stability of the structure. For more information on the use of pier blocks and concrete, refer to the foundation and floor fundamentals chapter in part 1.

· Project 1 ·

HIDEAWAY

The Hideaway, perfect for the small backyard and small budget, has 32 square feet of floor space and a shed roof (half a gable) with a 2-in-12, 9½-degree slope.

BUILDING THE FLOOR

The slope of the ground on which you plan to build the Hideaway will determine the foundation needs.

From pressure-treated stock, cut two stringers 96 inches long and five joists 45 inches long. Assemble and square the floor as described in part 1. When the floor frame is level and square, secure the flooring material with 8d galvanized nails or 1½-inch screws every 10 to 12 inches.

BUILDING THE WALLS

Snap chalk lines 4 inches in from the outside edges of the floor. Cut four plates 95 inches long for the front and back walls. Tack them to the floor in pairs along the lines. Cut four plates 40 inches long for the end walls and tack them to the floor. Lay out all the regular studs and the door and window openings.

Project 1 Materials List

Description	Quantity	Length in feet	Comments
4 × 4	1	8	Pressure-treated posts
2 × 6	5	8	Pressure-treated joists
2 × 4	6	8	Plates, sills, headers
2 × 4	2	10	Fascia
2 × 4	24	12	Studs, trimmers, rafters, etc.
1 × 2	1	12	Cedar rake mold
Pier blocks	6		
¾" flooring	1		Sheet, treated
½" sheathing	7		Sheets
Nails, screws			As needed

The front wall is 8 inches taller than the back and end walls. Front-wall studs are 61½ inches; all others are 53½ inches. To ensure a good fit, don't cut the trimmers until the headers are in place.

Erect and brace the walls. The difference in the height of the front and end walls precludes the use of doubler plates to tie the front wall to the end walls, as shown in Figure 1.3. Doubler plates will, however, cross-lap the back wall. Thus the doubler plate for the front wall is 95 inches and for the back wall 88 inches.

Sheath the front and back walls, first making sure they are plumb both ways at the corners.

BUILDING THE ROOF

Cut the rafters from straight, clear 2 × 4 stock. Refer to Figure 1.4 for length. Do not make seat cuts in the barge rafters. The barge rafters are supported by a pair of 2 × 4 fascia boards cut 108 inches long.

Lay out the rafters along the top of the walls. Toe-nail the rafters to the walls. To make sheathing the end walls easier, do so before installing the barge rafters.

Cut and nail in the bird blocks as shown in Figures 1.2 and 1.3.

Nail the fascia boards on the ends of the rafters as shown in Figure 1.2. The fascia on the low end must be dropped enough that the roof sheathing can make a smooth transition from the rafters to the outside corner of the fascia.

Nail down the roof sheathing using 7d or 8d nails about every 8 inches. For best results, use roll roofing with 1 × 3 flashing all around.

Flashing at the top of the roof should be applied on top of the roofing. Cover nail holes with roofing cement.

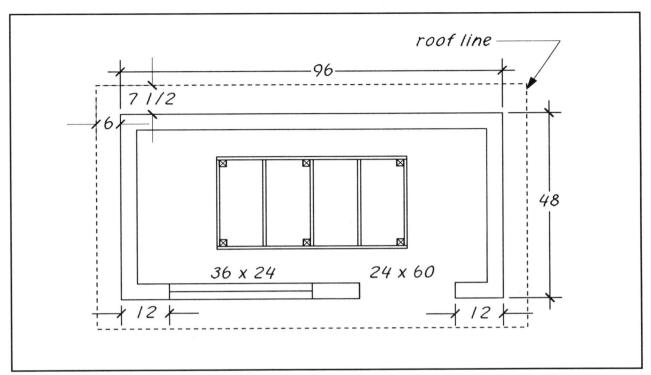

Figure 1.1. Plan view. Inset shows joist layout and post positions.

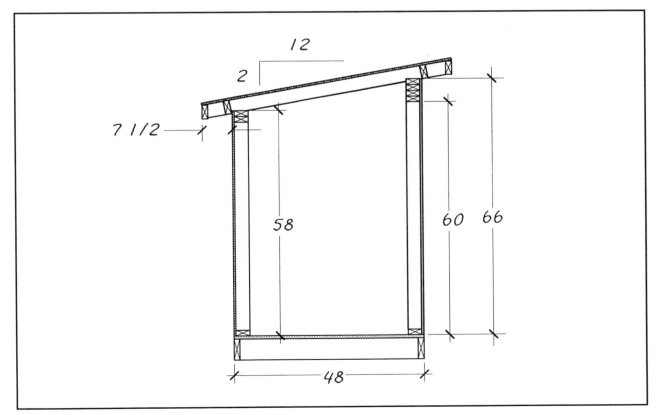

Figure 1.2. Section

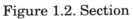

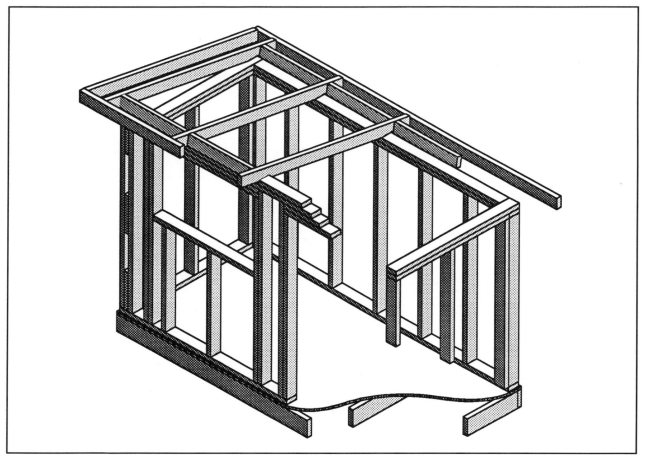

Figure 1.3. Framing plan

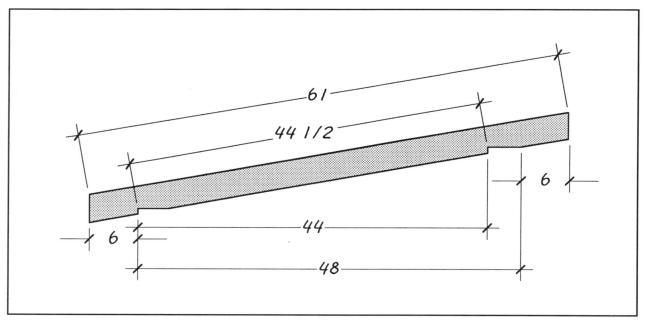

Figure 1.4. Rafter detail

▪ Project 2 ▪
BUNKHOUSE

The Bunkhouse is a large 80 square feet. The side windows are located well forward to accommodate a pair of bunks, perfect for summer sleep-outs with friends. The 6-in-12, 26½-degree roof has a gable extension over the 24×48 inch porch. The use of collar ties instead of joists gives an extra 6 inches of headroom down the center of the building.

BUILDING THE FLOOR

Carefully study the plans and materials list before beginning. Consider ground slope and other conditions to determine special needs.

Project 2 Materials List

Description	Quantity	Length in feet	Comments
4 × 4	1	8	Pressure-treated posts
4 × 4	1	8	Headers
2 × 6	6	8	Pressure-treated joists
2 × 6	3	10	Pressure-treated stringers, bridging
2 × 6	1	14	Ridge
2 × 4	20	8	Headers, sills, collar ties, misc.
2 × 4	6	10	Plates
2 × 4	34	12	Studs, rafters, fascias
2 × 4	5	8	Pressure-treated decking
1 × 2	2	12	Rake mold
Pier blocks	14		
¾" flooring	3		Sheets, treated
½" sheathing	12		Sheets
Nails, screws			As needed

From treated 2 × 6, cut two stringers 120 inches long and six joists 93 inches long. Assemble the floor as described in part 1 and as shown in Figure 2.2. Assemble the porch with treated 2 × 4s.

BUILDING THE WALLS

Snap chalk lines 4 inches in from the perimeter of the floor. Cut four plates 119 inches long and four plates 88 inches long. Tack the plates to the floor as described in part 1. Begin your layout at the left end of one of the side walls. Locate the 36 × 30 windows 12 inches in from the front corners. Center the back window and front door. The 18 × 30 windows are located just to the right and left of the door, the distance determined by the king studs and trimmers of each. Lay out the common studs 16 or 24 inches on center.

Count the number of studs you will need, and cut them 67½ inches long. Cut ten trimmers 58½ inches long. Each of the headers is 3 inches longer than its rough opening is wide. The headers for the 36-inch windows are 4 × 4, either built up or solid. The smaller windows have single 2 × 4s for headers. Two 2 × 4s nailed directly to the top plate form the header for the front door. Cut the other pieces as needed.

Nail together four corner posts, using pieces of scrap between two studs.

Set aside all but one set of side-wall plates. Lay the plates on the floor with the bottom plate near the edge of the floor and the top plate near the opposite edge. Face-nail the corners and studs into place, including the king studs for the windows. Nail the trimmers to the bottom plate and to their king studs. Nail in the headers, sills, and cripples, using 8d toe nails where necessary. Cut a doubler plate 112 inches long and nail it to the top plate, making sure it is 3½ inches in from each end.

Place the framed wall along the line, and measure the diagonals between the top and bottom plates; do not include the doubler plate. If necessary, tack the wall to the floor to keep it in place. Nail on the sheathing using 7d or 8d nails (galvanized if no siding will be applied later) spaced 8 to 10 inches. Transfer window measurements to the sheathing, and trim the openings with a circular saw. Lift the wall, and make sure it is located correctly before nailing it to the floor with 16d nails. Brace the wall at each end with a 2×4 nailed to the corner post and the outside of the floor. Let the wall lean outward an inch or so out of plumb so that it will not interfere with the raising of the end walls.

Build the opposite side wall before beginning the end walls. You will not be able to nail on the doubler plate or fully sheath the end walls before you raise them. Raise the end walls, and make sure that corners are plumb before nailing them together. Then nail on the 95-inch doubler plates and finish the sheathing.

BUILDING THE ROOF

Lay out the rafters along the top of the wall as described in part 1. Select a straight 2×4 to use as a rafter pattern. Refer to Figure 2.5 for barge and common rafter lengths, or step off the lengths as also described in part 1. Cut four barge rafters and twelve common rafters, noting that, because of the gable extension, the long barge rafters in the front are the same length as the common rafters but do not have seat cuts.

Next, lay out the 12-foot, 9-inch ridge board to correspond with the layout on the walls. Lean the common rafters against the side walls, and lay the ridge across the end walls. With the help of an assistant, nail a pair of rafters to one end of the ridge and then another pair to the other. Avoid beginning with the gable rafters to guard against a rafter accidentally slipping off the wall.

Check the fit of the seat cuts, and nail the rafters to the plates. Measure and cut a gable stud to support the ridge at each end. Plumb and brace the gable before nailing in the rest of the common rafters.

Cut two fascia boards 12 feet long. Mark the positions of the gable rafters on the fascias, and nail each to the rafter tails with galvanized nails. Notice in Figure 2.3 that the outside corner of the fascia—not the inside—is flush with the top edge of the rafters. Use a straightedge to get the alignment right.

Nail the barge rafters to the ridge at the peak and to the fascia at the bottom.

The barge rafters that form the extension at the front of the bunkhouse are held at the top by the ridge board and at the bottom by a pair of out hangers, as shown in Figure 2.4. Measure along the ridge from the end of the ridge board to the first common rafter. This is the length of the out hangers.

To locate the notches for the out hangers, measure down the gable and barge rafters 20½ inches and 24 inches, and draw lines square through the marks on the top edges. Set the depth of your circular saw to 1½ inches. Make several passes with the saw on and between the marks. Knock out the waste with a hammer, and clean up the bottom of the notches with a chisel.

Check to see that the barge rafter and gable rafter both are straight, then nail in the out hangers. Now you can install the short barge rafters and short fascia boards.

The collar ties are approximately 80 inches long and are cut at each end to correspond to the slope of the roof. Locate them 78 inches above the floor. Cut and install the remaining gable studs, and if you plan to cover the ceiling, add the necessary backing at the gables.

After nailing down the roof sheathing, install the 1×2 rake molding at the gable ends.

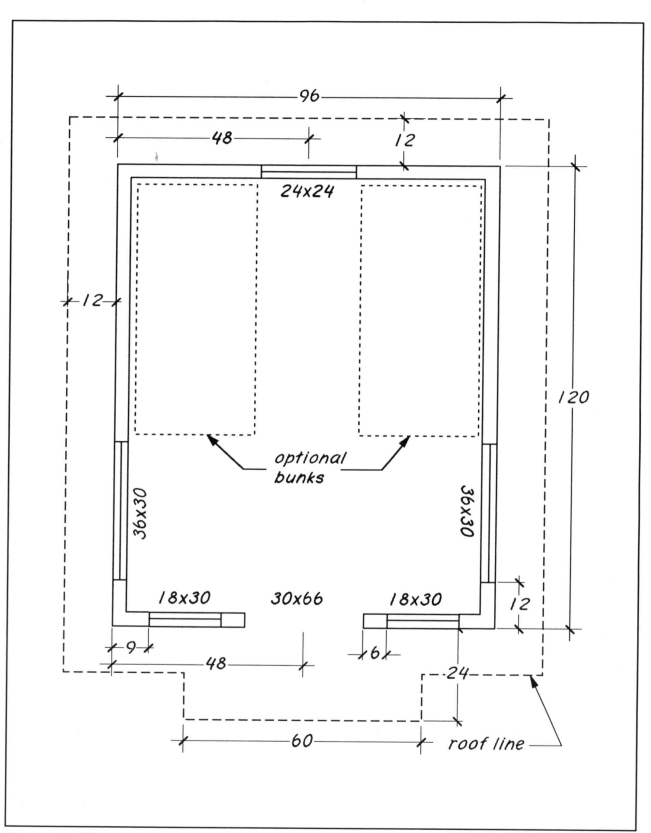

Figure 2.1. Plan view

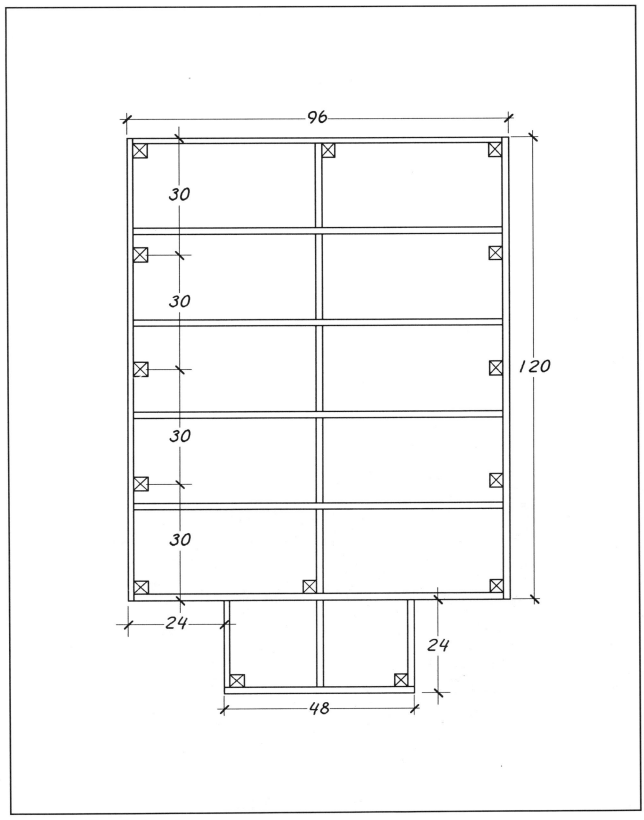

Figure 2.2. Foundation plan

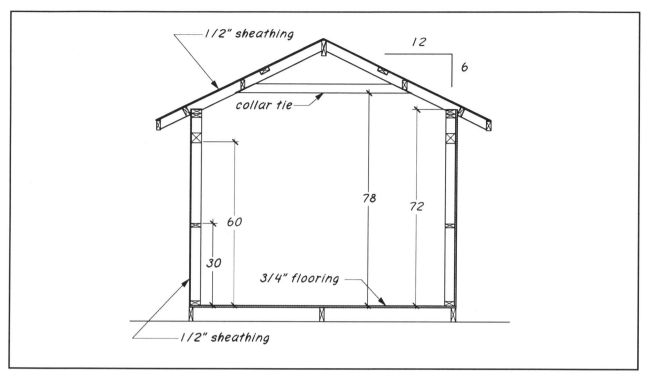

Figure 2.3. Section

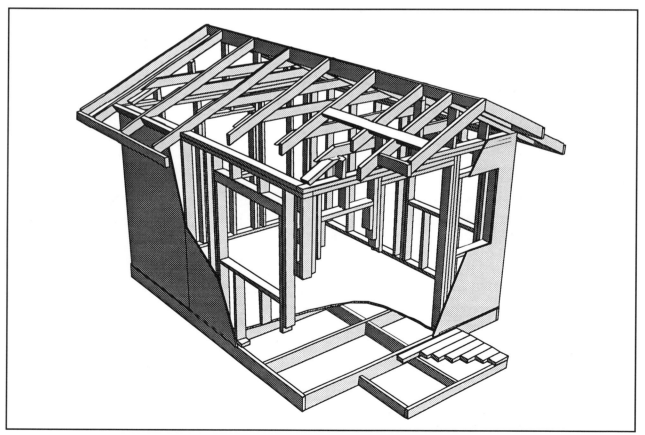

Figure 2.4. Framing plan

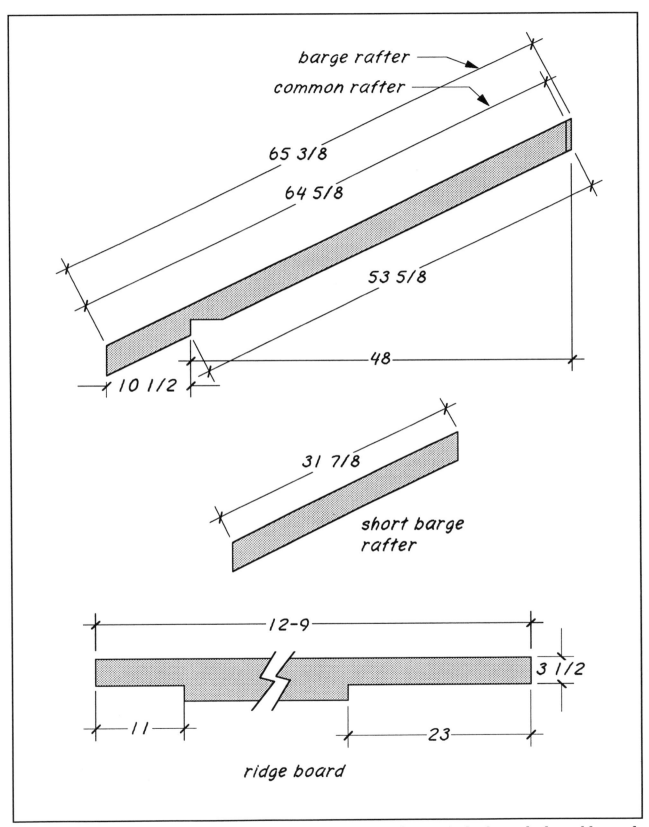

Figure 2.5. Rafters and ridge board. Note that the 2×6 ridge extends through the gables and supports the barge rafters. The ridge is cut back to the width of a 2×4 at each end.

· Project 3 ·

ALPINE A-FRAME

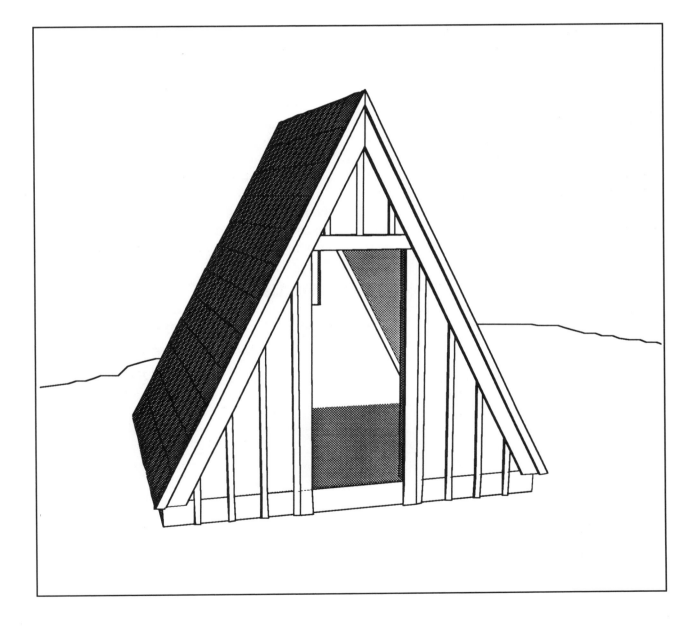

A-frames are easy and fast to build because roof and side walls are one and the same. Nestled neatly amid a grove of trees, its steep roof will easily shed needles, leaves, and snow. The Alpine A-Frame has 60 square feet of floor space and a 23½-in-12, 63-degree roof.

BUILDING THE FLOOR

Carefully study the plans and materials list before beginning. Consider ground slope and other conditions to determine special foundation needs.

From treated 2×6, cut two stringers 96 inches long and five joists 87 inches long. Assemble the floor as described in part 1 and as shown in Figure 3.2.

BUILDING THE ROOF

The roof is made of five trusses, as shown in Figures 3.3 and 3.4. You can build the trusses right on the floor. From straight #2 and better stock, cut ten rafters according to the dimensions given in Figure 3.5. Also cut ten plywood gussets. See Figure 3.3 for dimensions.

Lay a pair of rafters on the floor. Measure between the tails to ensure that they are 96 inches apart. Nail a few scraps to the floor to lock the rafters in place. Nail a gusset to the peak using 4d galvanized nails or 1½-inch roofing nails about every 2 inches. For extra strength, first apply a bead of construction adhesive. Flip the truss and apply a gusset to the other side.

Cut four plates 89 inches long. Nail two of them flush with the edge of the floor along the sides and ½ inch in from each end. The remaining two plates are for the end walls. Lay out the trusses 24 inches OC. Also at this time lay out the end walls, centering the door in the front wall and the window in the back wall.

Raise the rear truss, nail it to the plate, and firmly brace it plumb. Stack the other trusses against the gable.

Lay out a 2×4 or 1×4 to correspond with the plate. You will use this to locate and temporarily hold the trusses at the peak. Move the opposite gable (the top truss in the stack) and nail it in place at the front of the A-frame. Tack the temporary spacer

Project 3 Materials List

Description	Quantity	Length in feet	Comments
4×4	2	10	Pressure-treated posts
2×6	8	8	Pressure-treated joists, bridging
2×4	14	8	Plates, studs, miscellaneous
2×4	10	10	Rafters
1×8	2	8	Cedar fascia
1×6	4	10	Cedar barge board
1×2	4	10	Cedar rake mold
Pier blocks	10		
¾" flooring	2		Sheets, treated
½" sheathing	8		Sheets
Nails, screws			As needed

near the ridge, and place the rest of the trusses.

BUILDING THE END WALLS
Use a level and straightedge to transfer the layout of the end walls to the gable trusses. Header height is 60 inches.

Install 2×4 ceiling backing against the inside of each gable rafter, as shown in Figures 3.4 and 3.6. Then sheath the end walls.

To bring the roof slightly beyond the end walls, nail 2×4 spacers along the rake. Then nail the 1×6 barge boards onto the spacers.

Study the inset in Figure 3.3 and install the 1×8 cedar fascia as shown.

To complete the A-frame, install the roof sheathing and the 1×2 cedar rake mold.

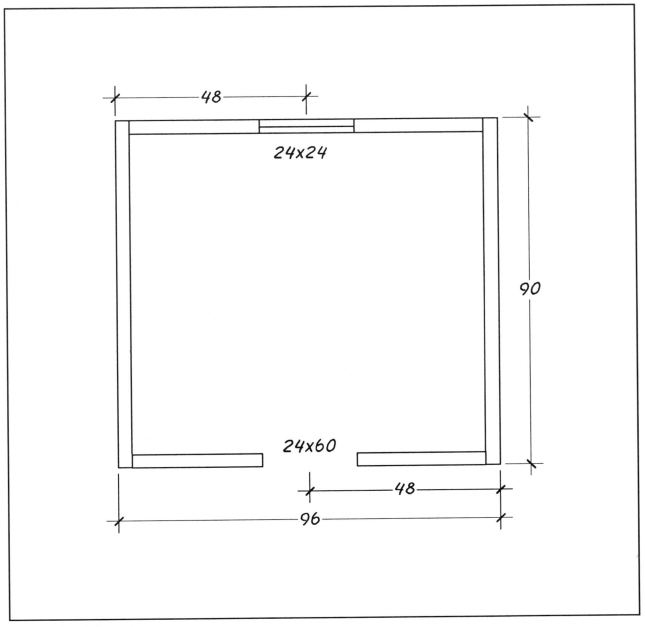

Figure 3.1. Plan view

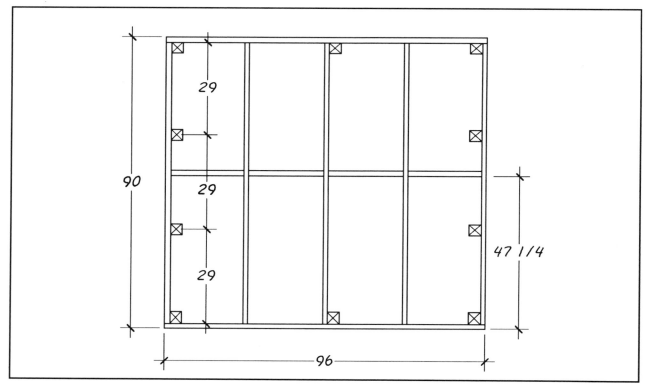

Figure 3.2. Foundation plan

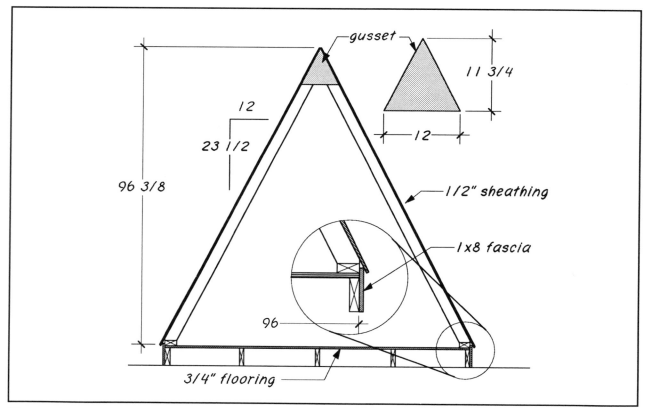

Figure 3.3. Section

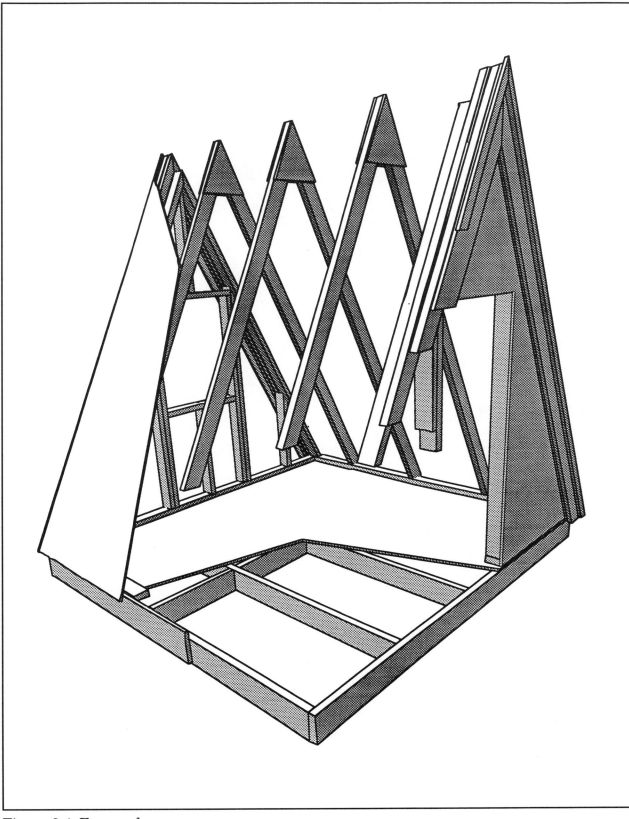

Figure 3.4. Frame plan

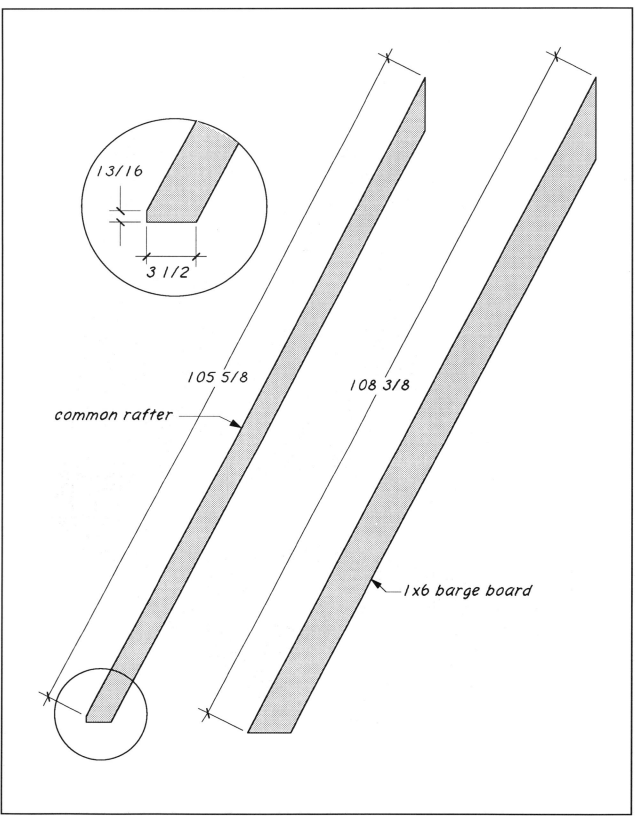

Figure 3.5. Rafter and barge board details

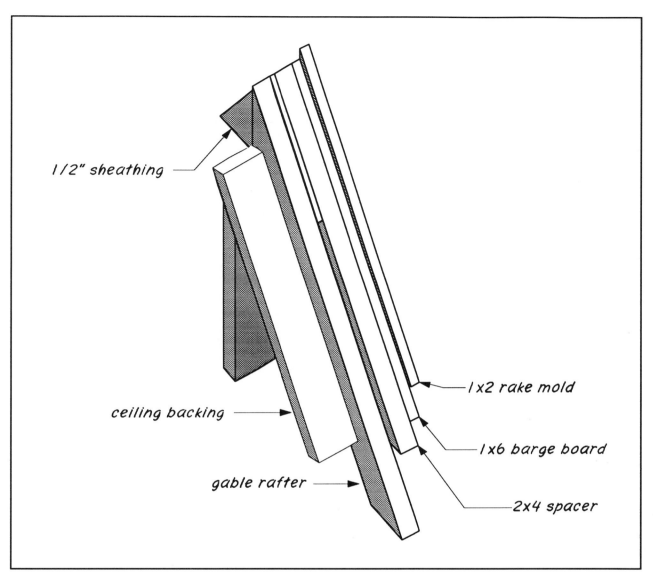

1/2" sheathing

ceiling backing

gable rafter

1x2 rake mold

1x6 barge board

2x4 spacer

Figure 3.6. Gable detail. Along the rake are nailed 2 × 4 spacers. They can be made of scraps or cut full length. Nail 1 × 6 cedar barge boards to the spacers. Siding slips easily behind the barge board. Rake mold covers the edge of the sheathing.

▪ Project 4 ▪
FORT FRONTIER

ort Frontier is a four-tiered climbing structure that stands 10 feet tall and covers 64 square feet. Each level is 2 feet higher than the one below it. The 2×2 balusters enclose the upper two tiers and form a "stockade" on level one.

SETTING THE POSTS

Use nine small stakes to roughly locate the posts. If necessary, set batter boards as described in part 1 to locate them precisely. Use a post-hole digger to dig holes about 2 feet deep, and wide enough to allow for easy adjustment. Set the posts in concrete for optimum stability. For safety, do not pour concrete above grade level, where a child could get scraped or cut.

Place the posts according Figure 4.1. It's unlikely that the posts will be at the correct height once they are set, so begin with posts longer than needed, and cut them to length as you work your way up.

Set the corner posts—1, 3, 5, and 7 in Figure 4.1—first. The other posts are easily located from these.

ASSEMBLING THE FORT

Refer to Figures 4.2, 4.3, and 4.4 for placement of the 3×6 stringers. Use three 16d galvanized nails or two or three 3-inch deck screws on each end of the stringer.

Install the level-one stringers first. The suggested elevation of level one is 12 inches; however, it can be built low enough that the 2×6 treated stringers are touching the ground. Use a hand saw to cut post 1 flush with the top of the stringers. Then screw or nail on the 2×6 decking, notching the boards around the posts. Nail pieces of 2×4 to the posts as backing if necessary. Use a 16d nail as a spacer between each decking board. Once the level-one decking is in place, subsequent vertical measurements can be taken from there.

Project 4 Materials List

Description	Quantity	Length in feet	Comments
4×4	4	12	Pressure-treated posts
4×4	3	10	Pressure-treated posts
4×4	1	8	Pressure-treated posts
2×6	11	10	Pressure-treated or cedar. Cut all pieces longer than 48" from 10' stock.
2×6	25	8	Pressure-treated or cedar
2×4	3	10	Pressure-treated or cedar. Cut all pieces longer than 48" from 10' stock.
2×4	3	8	PT or cedar
2×2	15	10	Cedar
2×2	18	8	Cedar
Concrete mix	9		Sacks
Nails, screws			As needed

With all the decking secured, and the posts cut to correct height, measure 1¾ inches down from the top of the posts, and draw lines square on all four sides of them. Set your circular saw at 45 degrees to bevel the posts. Making such cuts takes a firm, steady hand as well as a sharp saw. The cuts can be made in one direction only. Use extreme caution to avoid binding the blade,

saw kickback, and possible personal injury.

Affix the 2×4 rails with nails or screws 36 inches above the deck of each level. Also place the steps midway between the levels.

Next, lay out the balusters at 6 inches OC. Cut them to length, then cut a 45-degree bevel on the top end. Secure the balusters with 10d galvanized finish nails or screws.

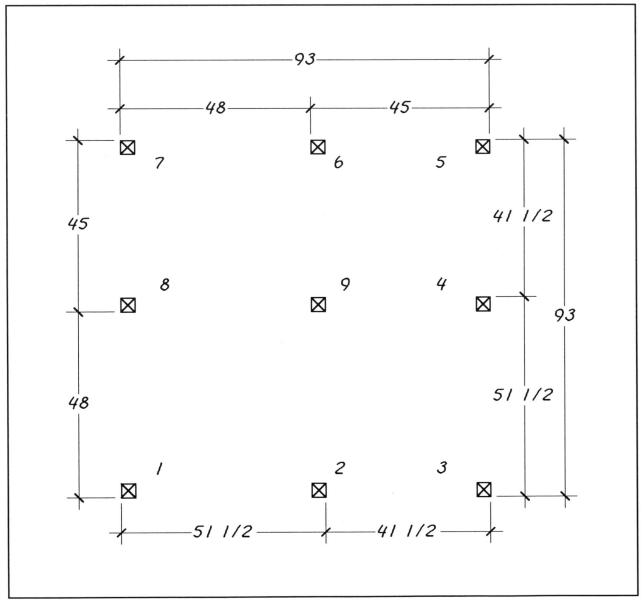

Figure 4.1. Post layout

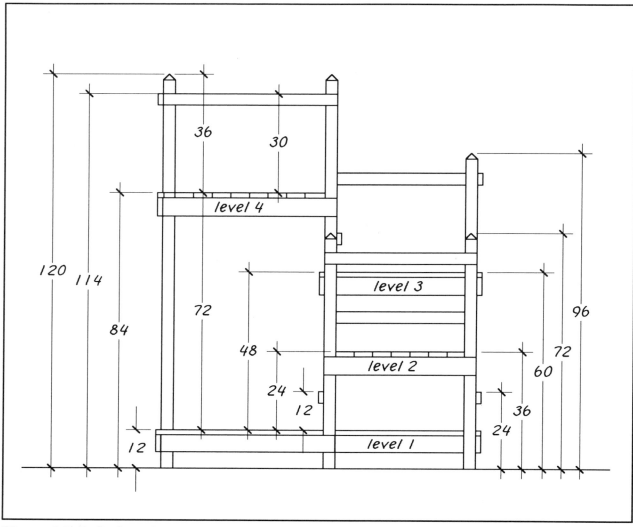

Figure 4.2. Left elevation

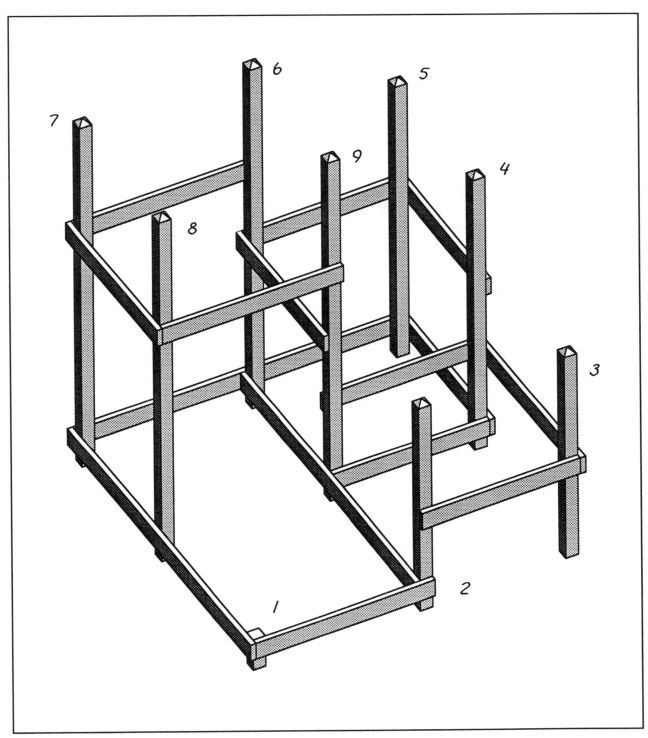

Figure 4.3. Stringer detail

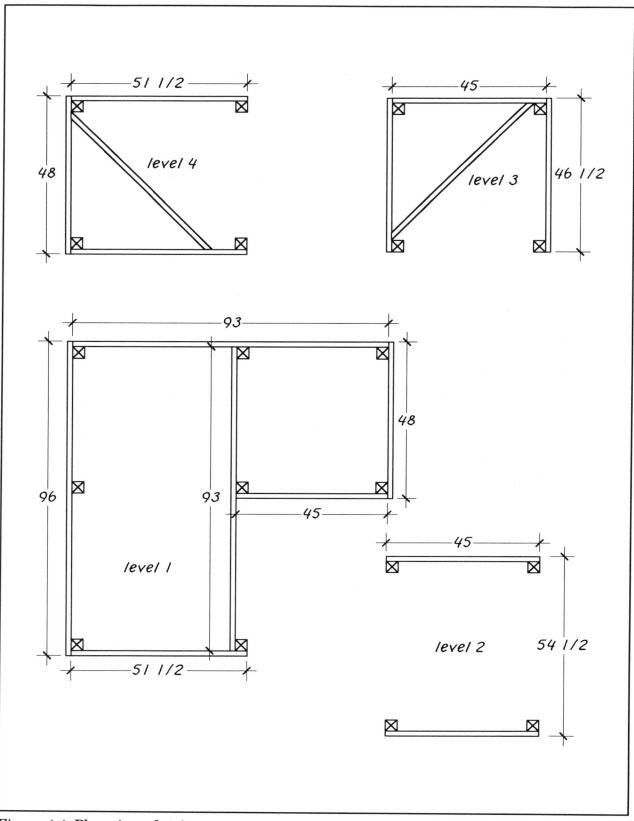

Figure 4.4. Plan view of stringers

· Project 5 ·

COVERED BRIDGE WITH SWING AND POLE

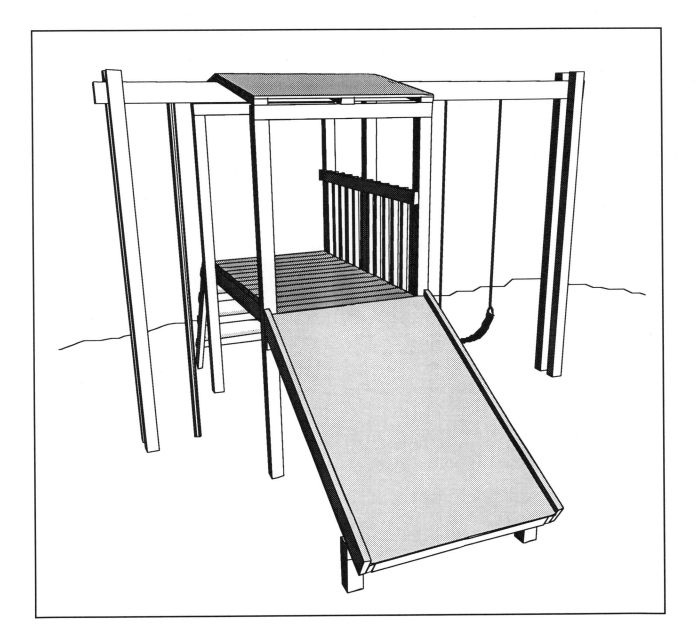

The Covered Bridge features a swing on one side and a fire pole on the other. The bridge is accessible by an angled ladder at the back and a ramp at the front. The ramp consists of a sheet of ¾-inch plywood over a frame, and several treatments are within the grasp of the do-it-yourselfer. You can nail 1×2 cleats horizontally and spaced about 12 inches apart for traction, or you can coat the surface with a readily available rubberized, textured material. Alternatively, you can convert the ramp to a slide by covering the surface with a sheet of stainless steel, taking care that all sharp edges are concealed, or replace the ramp with a manufactured slide.

All posts are pressure-treated. The remaining materials should be cedar, redwood, or treated fir.

If you have the room, consider replacing the ladder with the monkey bars unit described in project 14.

SETTING THE POSTS AND BEAMS

The main beam and the double posts at each end form the primary support structure and are installed first. Lay out and dig the post holes as shown in Figures 5.1 and 5.2. The bottom of the beam is 8 feet, 6 inches from the ground. Because the beam is bolted to the posts before raising, be sure the holes are deep enough to allow for horizontal adjustment.

Cut the beam 13 feet long, and locate the posts 3 inches in from each end. Bore ⅝-inch-diameter holes as shown in Figure 5.4. At this time you can also bore the holes in the beam for the other hardware, as indicated in Figure 5.2.

Lay the posts and beam roughly in place on the ground, and bolt the assembly together. You will need to install 4×4 spacers near the bottom ends of the posts. (If the spacers are pressure-treated, they may also be planted in the post holes.) Use two long 2×4s to brace the posts at right angles to the beam. Before raising the beam, have plenty of bracing material on hand. Lift the beam (it will take two people) and brace it. Make sure the posts are plumb and equidistant at the bottom and the beam is level. Mix and pour the cement, working it well around the posts. If it was necessary to raise the posts on either end from the bottom of the hole to level the beam, be sure to work sufficient cement or gravel under the posts.

Locate the position of the center post along the beam. Then use a plumb line or a long straightedge with a level to locate the hole for the center post. Nail a post cap to the end of the center post, then secure the post to the beam. Brace the bottom of the post plumb in both directions, and fill the hole with concrete mix.

The remaining posts are located relative to the center post. For best results, make sure the bridge structure is perpendicular to the beam. Do not worry about the height of the posts when installing them; they can be cut just prior to setting the beams. The tops of the 4×4 bridge beams are 6 inches lower than the top of the main beam. Attach the beams to the posts with post caps.

The location and height of the posts and beam that support the ramp at the bottom will leave the lower edge of the ramp about 12 inches from the ground.

BUILDING THE BRIDGE

Locate and mount the 4×6 bridge timbers as shown in Figures 5.2 and 5.3. Use two ½×6-inch bolts with washers at each post. For safety, the bolts must be counterbored on the outside. Cut sufficient decking boards 41 inches long, and nail or screw them to the timbers. Nail or screw the 2×4 rail to the posts, with its top edge 30 inches from the deck. Use 8d galvanized nails to secure the balusters to the rail and bridge timbers.

Roof construction (Figure 5.5) requires no special cutting or fitting. Simply mea-

Project 5 Materials List

Description	Quantity	Length in feet	Comments
4 × 4	9	12	Treated posts
4 × 4	2	8	Treated short posts, short beams
4 × 6	1	14	Main beam
4 × 6	1	12	Deck beams
2 × 4	8	8	Ladder, ramp frame, rafters
2 × 4	3	12	Ladder, ramp frame
2 × 6	7	8	Decking
2 × 6	1	12	Ramp skirts
2 × 2	6	8	Balusters
¾" plywood	1		Sheet
½" plywood	1		Sheet
Pipe	1	10	2" diameter
Swing hardware			Specialty item, see text
Post caps	7		
Concrete mix	11		Sacks
Nails, screws			As needed
Bolts with nuts and washers	4		½" × 11½"
Bolts with nuts and washers	10		½" × 6"

sure from the center of the main beam to the outside edge of the bridge beam to determine rafter length. The ends are cut square. Use 16d galvanized nails or deck screws to secure the rafters to the beams. Use 5d galvanized nails or 1¼-inch screws to secure the plywood roof. No roofing materials are required, but if you caulk the seam at the ridge and apply two or three coats of house paint to the top surface and edges, the roof will last longer.

Measurements given for the ladder in Figure 5.6 are approximate. Use the post as a guide to mark the angle at the upper end of the rails. Use screws to mount the rungs and to secure the ladder to the posts.

To build the ramp, first make a frame from 2 × 4s 45 inches wide and 69 inches long, as shown in Figure 5.7. Rest the lower end of the frame on the support beam. The elevation of the ledger is approximate. With the upper end against the posts, use a piece of ¾-inch stock as an aid in locating the frame so that the finished height will be flush with the deck. Then use a piece of 2 × 4 stock underneath to mark the location of the ledger. Screw the ledger into place. Center the frame and nail it into place. Next, cut and nail down the ¾-inch plywood ramp to the frame with 7d galvanized nails.

Use the posts as a guide to mark the angle at the upper end of the 2 × 6 skirt boards. Nail these into place at the posts and to the frame.

INSTALLING THE HARDWARE

There are a number of ways to hang a swing and several kinds of hardware, from rope to chain, eyebolts to bearings, flexible rubber seat to a chunk of 2×6. Check your Yellow Pages under "Playground Equipment" for local outlets of specialty hardware.

To mount the fire pole, bore a hole on the underside of the beam just slightly larger than the outside diameter of the pipe (Figure 5.8). Make the hole at least 2 inches deep. Dig a hole in the ground about 12 inches deep and 8 inches in diameter. Cut the pipe about 3 inches shorter than the distance between the bottoms of the holes in the ground and the beam. Fill the hole in

the ground with concrete mix. Push the pipe into the concrete and move it around to ensure that plenty of concrete works its way into and underneath the pipe. Then lift the pipe and push it into the hole in the beam. Secure the pole at the beam with an 8d galvanized nail or a ¼×2-inch lag bolt, as shown in Figure 5.8, first boring an appropriate diameter hole through the beam and into the pole. The fastener will keep the pole from twisting and will allow it to hang as the concrete sets up. Periodically check that the pole remains plumb in both directions. The top of the concrete should be below grade level so that it will not present a hazard to children.

Spread 6 to 10 inches of resilient material, such as bark chips, around the play area.

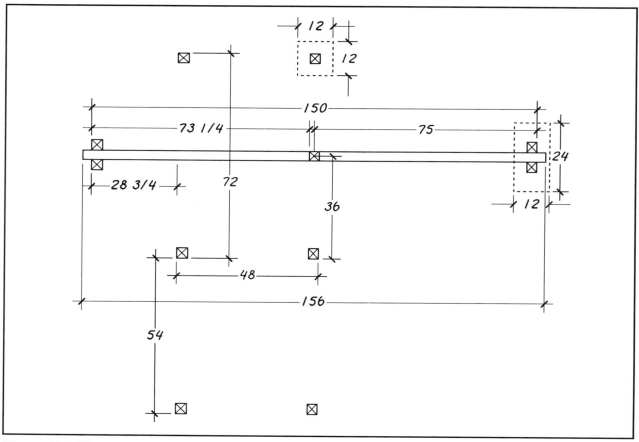

Figure 5.1. Plan view of post layout

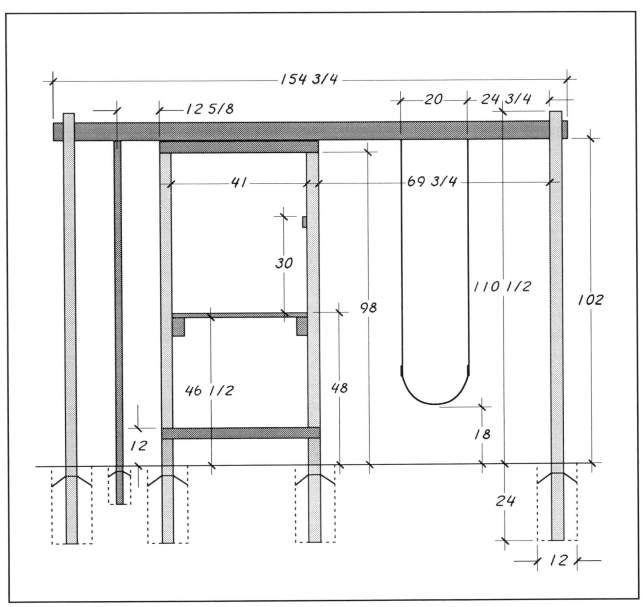

Figure 5.2. Front elevation (roof, ramp, ladder removed for clarity)

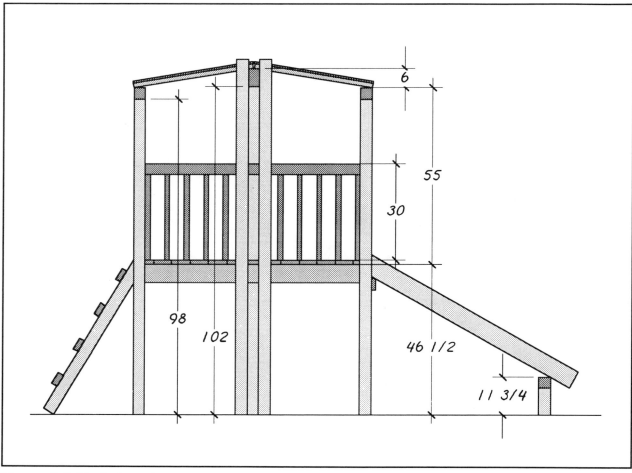

Figure 5.3. End elevation

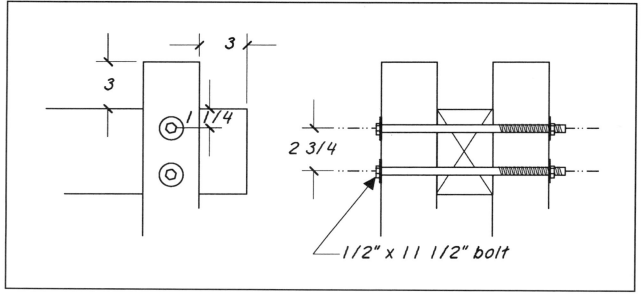

Figure 5.4. Bolt detail at main beam

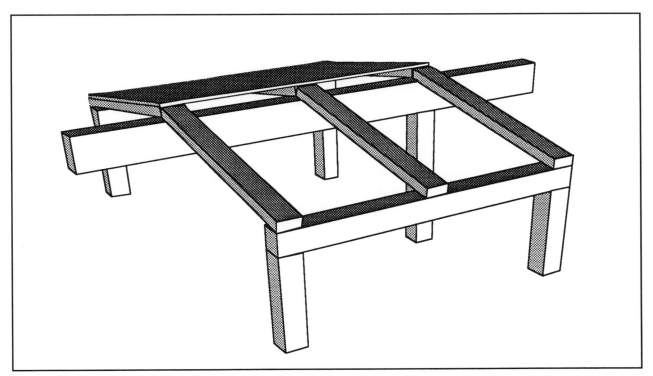

Figure 5.5. Roof detail

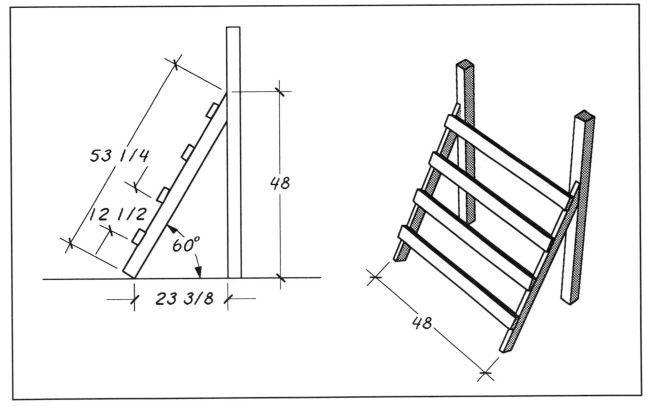

Figure 5.6. Ladder detail

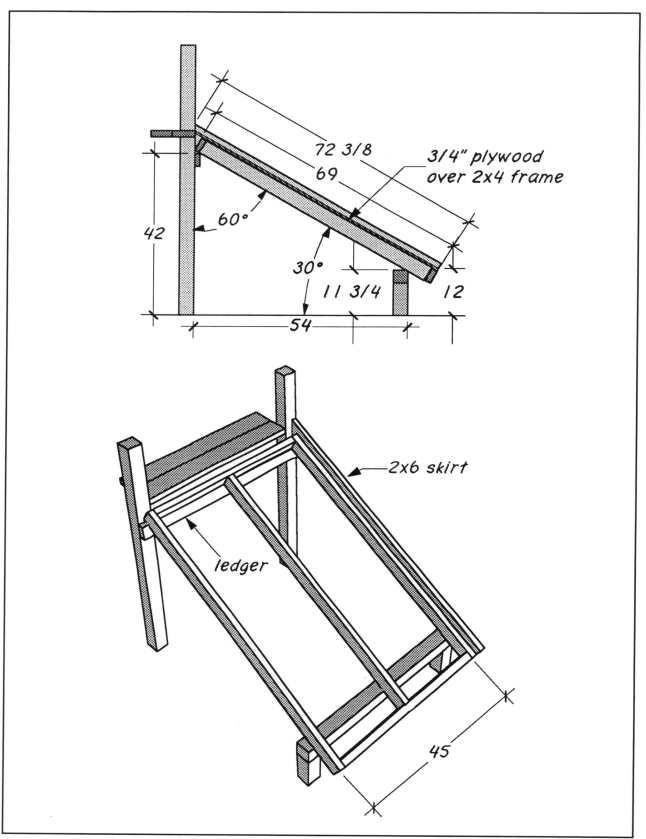

Figure 5.7. Ramp detail

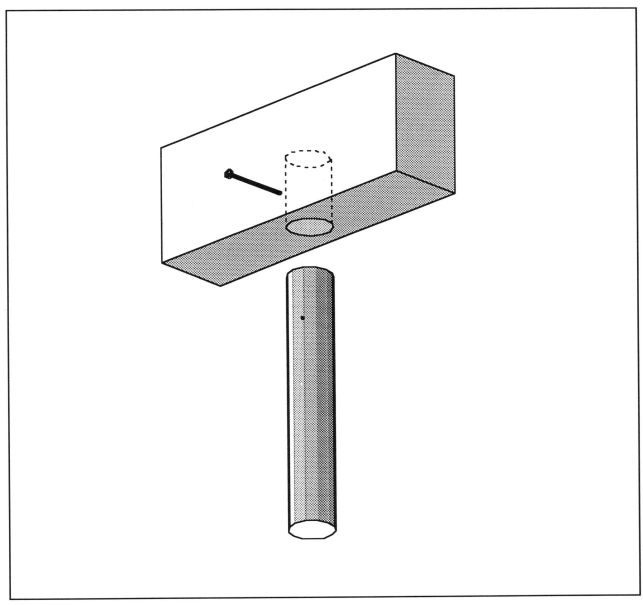

Figure 5.8. Pole detail

· Project 6 ·
KATIE'S COTTAGE

Katie's Cottage has 36 square feet of floor area. The 6-in-12, 21½-degree trussed roof extends over an 18-square-foot porch. The porch is enclosed with a 30-inch balustrade.

BUILDING THE FLOOR

Carefully study the plans and materials list before beginning. Consider ground slope and other conditions to determine special foundation needs.

From treated 2×6, cut two stringers 72 inches long and four joists 69 inches long. Assemble the floor as described in part 1 and as shown in Figure 6.2. Also install the porch stringer (72 inches long) and joists (34½ inches long). The joists for the main floor are set 24 inches on center, but the porch joists are set to accommodate the posts, as shown.

BUILDING THE WALLS

Snap chalk lines 4 inches in from the perimeter of the floor. Cut four plates 71 inches long for the front and back walls and four plates 64 inches long for the side walls. Tack the plates to the floor as described in part 1.

Lay out the door and window in the front wall using the measurements shown in Figure 6.1. The door and window are separated by the 6 inches formed by the combined king studs and trimmers. The 30×36 windows are centered in the side walls.

Count the number of studs you will need, and cut them 67½ inches long. Cut eight trimmers 58½ inches long. Each of the headers is 3 inches longer than its rough opening is wide. The headers in the front, nonbearing wall can be 2×4 or 4×4. The headers in the side walls should be

Project 6 Materials List

Description	Quantity	Length in feet	Comments
4×4	2	8	Pressure-treated posts
4×4	3	10	Pressure-treated porch posts
2×6	7	6	Pressure-treated stringers, bridging, joists
2×4	7	12	Presure-treated porch components
2×4	10	8	Top chords, headers, sills, cripples
2×4	4	10	Fascia, long plates
2×4	24	12	Studs, trimmers, bottom chords
2×4	3	8	Cedar porch rails, misc.
2×2	5	8	Cedar balusters
1×2			Cedar rake mold
Pier blocks	12		
¾" flooring	2		Sheets, treated
½" sheathing	11		Sheets
Nails, screws			As needed

4 × 4, either built up or solid. Cut the other pieces as needed.

Build the two posts for the back wall as described earlier. The posts for the front wall, however, are modified to form a pocket for the 2 × 6 porch beam (Figures 6.4, 6.5, 6.7, and 6.8). The outer member should be 63 ½ inches long, or 4 inches shorter than the studs. When building the front wall, it is important to get the posts located correctly on the top plate.

The floor is just big enough that you can build each wall one at a time. Build the back wall first. Separate the plates and lay them edge up on the floor. Nail in the corner posts and studs. Cut a doubler plate 64 inches long, and nail it to the top plate 3 ½ inches in from each end. Square the wall by measuring the diagonal dimensions. Do not include the doubler plate in the measurements. If necessary, tack the wall to the floor to keep it in place. Nail on the sheathing using 7d or 8d nails (galvanized if you will not be applying siding later) spaced 8 to 10 inches apart.

Set the wall aside and begin the front wall. Face-nail the corners and studs into place, including the king studs for the windows. Nail the trimmers to the bottom plate and to their king studs. Nail in the headers, sills, and cripples, using 8d toe nails where necessary. Cut a doubler plate 88 inches long, and nail it to the top plate. Square the wall and sheath it. Set the wall aside.

Build the side walls, but do not nail on the doubler plates or any sheathing. Set the walls in place on the floor, and anchor them with 16d nails driven into the joists and stringers every 16 to 24 inches. True up the corners, temporarily bracing the side walls, and nail them together.

Next, using a straightedge and level, mark the tops of the porch posts. The posts will be the same height as the top of the walls *without* the doubler plates (Figure

6.7). Notch the posts to receive the beams, and cut the posts to length.

Cut two lengths of 2 × 6 38 ½ inches. Notch one end of each to fit into the beam pockets in the front wall. Nail the beams into place. Use 10d galvanized nails to fasten the beams to the posts. Then nail down the doubler plates, which extend from the back wall to the posts.

Finally, sheath the side walls.

BUILDING THE ROOF

Refer to Figure 6.6 for the dimensions of the top and bottom chords and the gussets. The cut for the bottom chords is a level cut—that is, the line is marked against the body of the framing square set at 6-in-12. You can build the trusses right on the floor, provided you do so before raising the walls. Carefully lay out the shape of the truss and place a set of chords. Use scrap 2 × 4s to make a jig to lock the chords into place. Nail the gussets into place with 4d galvanized nails or 1 ½-inch roofing nails about 2 inches apart. For added strength, apply a bead of construction adhesive. Flip the truss and nail the gussets on the other side. Do not use gussets on the outside of the gable trusses, as they will interfere with the sheathing.

Lay out the trusses 24 inches on center. The truss that fits over the porch can be centered in the porch span. Lay out a 2 × 4 or 1 × 4 to correspond with the plate layout and to use as a temporary spacer. The spacer should be long enough to include the barge rafters at both ends. Nail and brace the gable rafters into place, and then bring in the other rafters. Use the temporary spacer to hold the trusses at the peak. Install bird blocks over the enclosed area, and ceiling backing along the tops of the end walls.

The gable overhang is 6 inches, and the barge rafters are held in place at the tails by a 2×4 fascia. Use a 120-inch fascia at the back and a pair of 36-inch fascias at the front, letting the ends run wild. Locate the fascia so that the outside corner—not the inside corner—is flush with the top surface of the rafters (Figure 6.3). Because of the short overhang, the roof sheathing in adequate to support the barge rafter, provided that it extends into the body of the roof.

The barge rafters are the same length as the top chords of the trusses. Once the barge rafters are nailed into place, trim off the ends of the fascia boards.

After nailing on the sheathing, install the rake molding at the gable ends.

BUILDING THE PORCH

Notch the 2×4 treated decking boards around the posts, working from the outside in. Use backing around the posts if necessary. Install the boards, using a 16d nail as a spacer. Cut the top of the short posts 28 1/2 inches above the porch floor. Do not build the railings until after any trim and siding are installed. It may be necessary to recalculate some dimensions and notch the side rails around corner boards.

Toe-nail the rails in place with 8d galvanized finish nails, or use galvanized fence clips. The ends of the top front rails are face-nailed to the posts.

Cut eighteen 2×2 balusters 21 inches long. Refer to Figures 6.7 and 6.8 for spacing details. The addition of siding will have an effect on the spacing of the side rails. Toe-nail the balusters into place with 8d galvanized finish nails. Predrill the holes, and set the nails with a nail set.

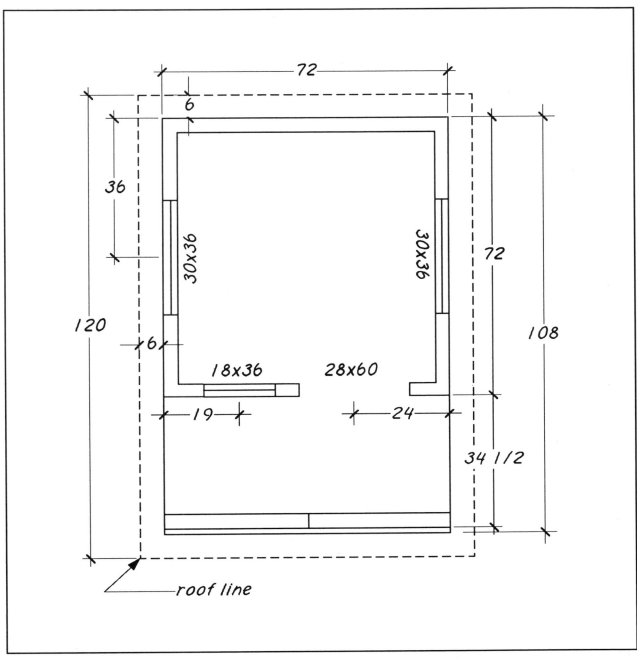

Figure 6.1. Plan view

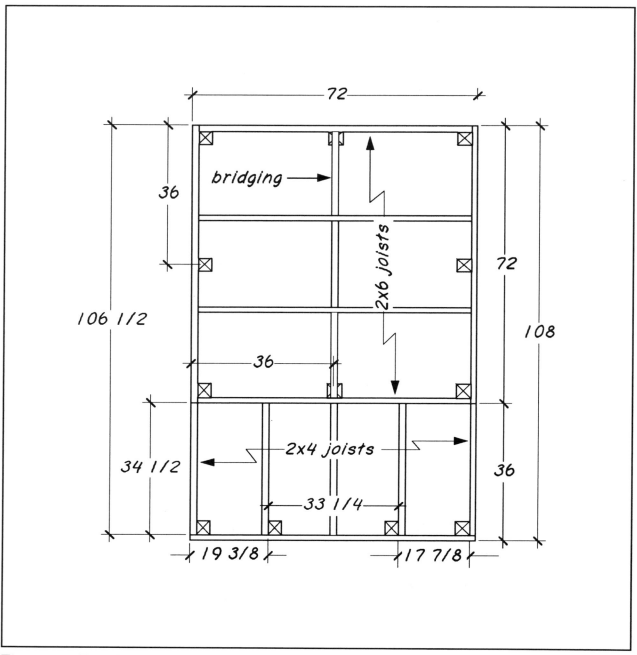

Figure 6.2. Foundation plan

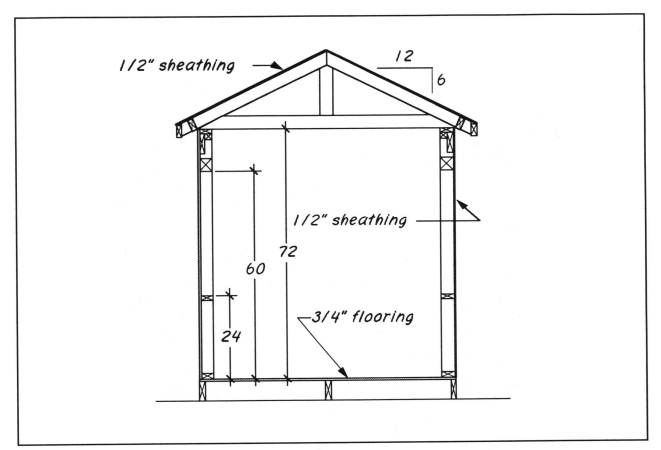

Figure 6.3. Section

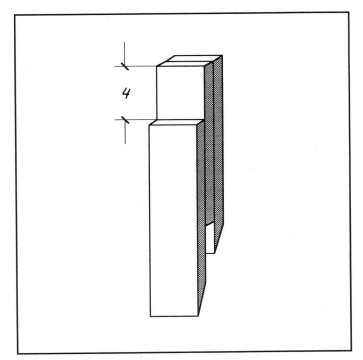

Figure 6.4. Front-wall corner-post details

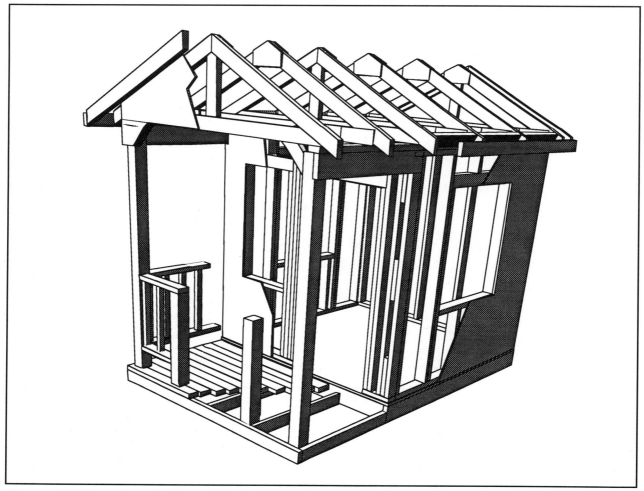

Figure 6.5. Framing plan

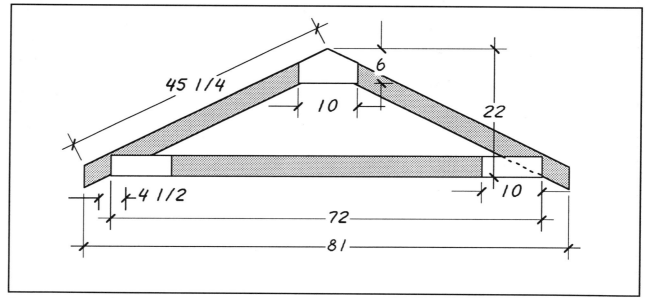

Figure 6.6. Truss detail

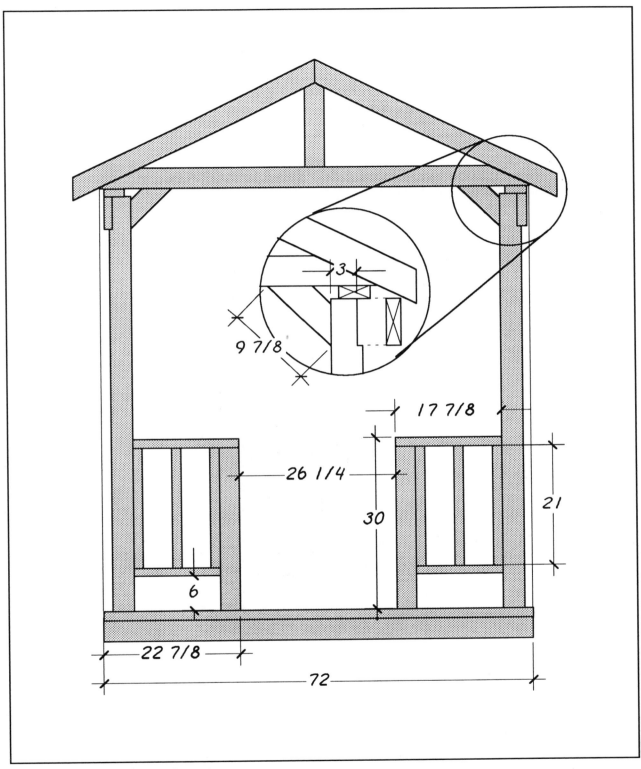

Figure 6.7. Porch front elevation

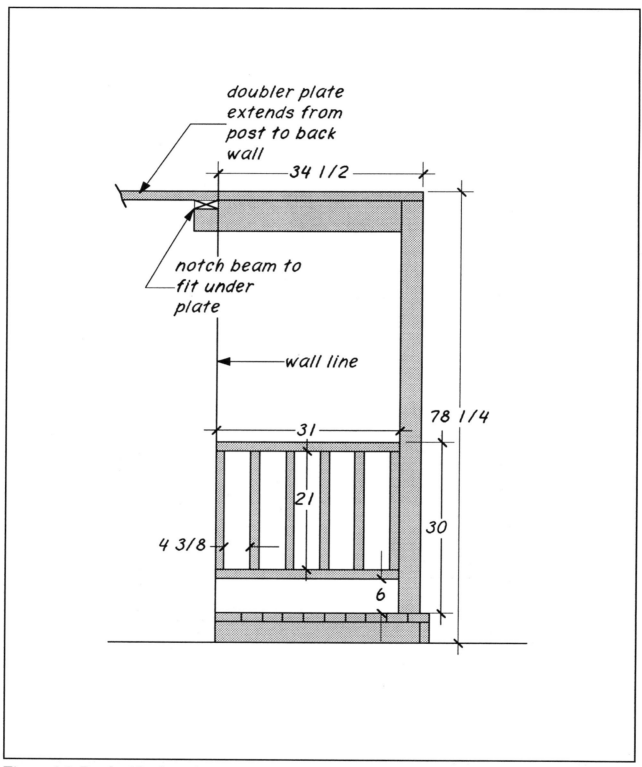

Figure 6.8. Porch side elevation

CASCADE FIRE TOWER

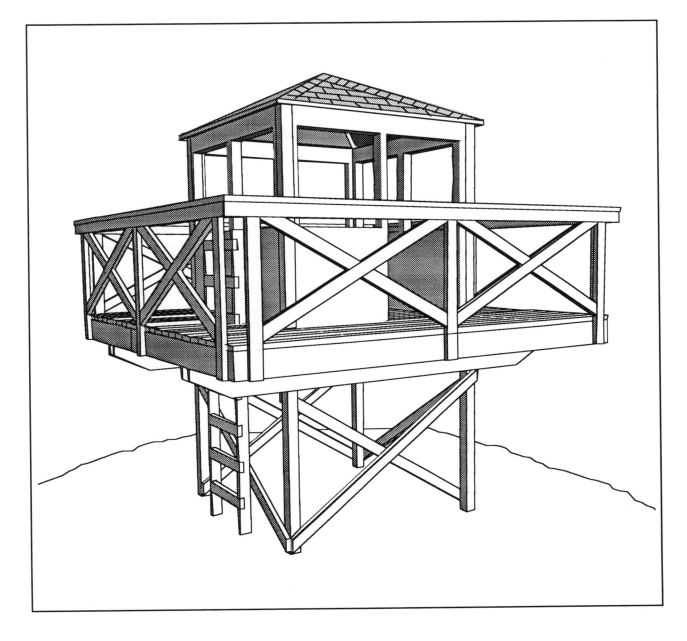

The Cascade Fire Tower is based on an actual design of fire towers used by members of the Forest Service in the mountains of the Pacific Northwest. The 11-foot-square deck is nearly 6 feet off the ground and is supported by four well-braced 4×4 posts, which also support the 6-in-12, 22½-degree hip roof. The cabin area is 36 square feet.

BUILDING THE MAIN STRUCTURE

The main structure consists of the posts and their braces, 2×10 stringers, 2×8 joists and stringers, and 2×6 decking. The posts support the deck and roof, and also frame the cabin walls. So that the rafters will fit accurately, the posts must be plumb and square; take care when laying them out and setting them. For best results, use batter boards, as described in part 1. Set the posts 6 feet apart in both directions (Figures 7.2 and 7.3) in holes 24 to 30 inches deep. Use temporary braces to hold the posts in place while you check the various dimensions. When the posts are plumb, parallel, and square, fill the holes with concrete. Do not pile the concrete higher than grade level; doing so may present a hazard to children. Also pour a 24×30-inch concrete pad as a base for the ladder.

After the concrete has set up, cut the 2×10 stringers 11 feet long, and chamfer the ends as shown in Figure 7.3. Lay out the posts, and mark the locations of the bolts on the stringers. You will use three ½×8½-inch bolts with washers on each post. Tack blocks to the posts on which to rest the stringers. Set the stringers on the blocks, and use one or two nails to hold the stringers in place. Now bore holes for the bolts. Bolt the stringers in place, and nail on the braces.

Next, install the deck system, beginning with the two 2×8 joists that fit against the

Project 7 Materials List

Description	Quantity	Length in feet	Comments
4×4	4	14	Pressure-treated posts
2×10	4	12	Cedar stringers
2×8	7	12	Cedar joists, stringers
2×8	1	4	Cedar headers (for ladder opening)
2×6	24	12	Cedar decking
2×4	24	12	Fir or cedar cabin frame
2×4	19	12	Cedar railing, braces, ladder
1×4	8	12	Cedar skirt for railing
½" sheathing	8		Sheets
Bolts with nuts and washers	12		½"×8½"
Nails, screws			As needed
Concrete mix	4		Sacks

posts. Ensure that they are located correctly before nailing them into place. Lay out the 2×8 stringers (which will fit on the ends of the joists). Tack the stringers into place, and set the remaining joists. Then nail the stringers firmly to the joists.

Sight down the length of the end joists to see if they are straight. If not, nail a 2×4 across the joists to hold them in place. Cut and install a pair of 2×8 headers to form the opening for the ladder.

Working from one end to the other, install the 2×6 decking using 16d galvanized nails or deck screws. To ensure that the ends of the boards won't split while fastening, let the ends run wild, and trim them off later. Space the boards about the thickness of a 16d nail. As you progress, check the remaining distance at each end to ensure that the boards are running even and that you won't end up with a narrow space to fill. Over a long span, you can adjust the spacing to end up with a full 2×6, 2×4, or 2×2 so that no ripping will be necessary.

BUILDING THE CABIN WALLS AND ROOF

Before building the cabin, trim the tops of the posts to 66 inches above the deck.

Framing the cabin walls is a simple matter of filling in between the posts. You can build the walls either on the floor or in place. If the posts are not plumb, it will be easier to build them in place and adjust the openings as necessary.

For each of the walls except the front, cut two plates 65 inches, four studs 63 inches, four headers $29\frac{1}{2}$ inches, four sill cripples 27 inches, and four header cripples 3 inches long. Nail them into place as shown in Figure 7.3. For the front wall, the bottom plate is 34 inches long and the rightmost door stud is $64\frac{1}{2}$ inches long. The stud rests directly on the deck. Use a straightedge to align the wall correctly between the posts.

Cover the walls with sheathing or plywood siding.

The first step in building the roof is to make the king post (Figure 7.4). The king post forms a solid, flat surface to which you will nail the rafters (Figure 7.6). Use a 6-inch piece of 4×4 planed or sawed to an octagon. It's best to begin with a longer piece and cut it to length once the dimensions are right. Note that each face of the king post is $1\frac{3}{8}$ inches wide, at least $\frac{1}{8}$ inch narrower than the 2×4 rafters are thick. Use a block plane to bevel the plumb cuts of each rafter.

Cut the common rafters according to the dimensions shown in Figure 7.6. The length given will allow the rafter to extend $1\frac{1}{2}$ inches from the plate line. At the tail, the length of the level cut is relative to the plumb cut. The length of the plumb cut at the tail should be at least $1\frac{1}{2}$ inches.

Toe-nail two rafters to the king post. Center the rafter tails on the walls, and tack them in place. You may have to prop the king post temporarily. Mount the other two common rafters, checking the fit all around.

The hip rafters are longer and rise to the peak at a 45-degree angle to the common rafters. They require different cuts than the common rafters. See Figure 7.7 for details. Notice that the length of the plumb cut at the tail is shorter than that on the common rafters. This will lower the hip rafters so that the upper corners along the rake will be flush with the planes of the roof line established by the common rafters. If the hip rafters were not lowered, the corners would need to be beveled—called a backing cut—to conform to the roof planes, which meet at the centerline of the hip rafters.) Check the hip rafters by tacking two in place and running a straightedge down the roof. The straightedge should ride along the corners of the hips and along the edge of the common rafter. The tails also must be beveled, as shown by the side cut in Figure 7.7.

Figure 7.7 also shows how to set the square to cut the sheathing at the correct angle. Install the sheathing and the optional 1 × 2 cedar fascia.

BUILDING THE LADDER AND RAILING

Install siding and trim before installing the ladder.

Build the ladder according to the dimensions given in Figure 7.8, notching the uprights to receive the 2 × 4 rungs. Cut the rungs slightly shorter than the deck opening is wide. To make the notches, clamp the uprights together and lay out the rungs. Set your saw to 1½ inches, and make passes about ¼ inch apart through each location. Separate the uprights, and knock out the waste with a hammer. Clean up the notches with a chisel. Use screws to fasten the rungs to the uprights. Put the ladder in place in the deck opening, and screw the uprights to the headers.

Refer to Figure 7.3 for the location of the 43½-inch balusters. Use screws or 16d galvanized nails to mount them.

The cross braces are on the same plane as the balusters, so they must be half-lapped at their intersections. Hold a length of 2 × 4 in place across the balusters and mark the ends. Cut the angles, and tack the brace in place. Hold another length of 2 × 4 across the balusters and the first brace. Mark the ends and the intersection, remembering to mark the intersection on the first brace as well. Take both braces down. Set the depth of your circular saw to ¾ inch and saw out the waste at the intersections. Fit the braces together, and secure them with 7d galvanized nails clinched over or 1¼-inch screws. Toe-nail the assembled braces to the balusters with 8d galvanized finish nails.

For the railing, center a 12-foot 2 × 4 on one set of balusters and nail it down. Center another 2 × 4 adjacent to and overlapping the first. Mark the inside and outside intersections on both pieces, and cut the angles on each piece accordingly (the angles should be 45 degrees). Nail the rail in place. Repeat the process for the other sides. Finally, secure the 1 × 4 cedar skirts beneath the rail inside and outside the balusters. Drive several 8d galvanized finish nails through the top of the rail into the skirt, taking care that the nails do not split out the side.

For safety, cordon off the ladder well with a length of rope or chain, or install a hinged trapdoor.

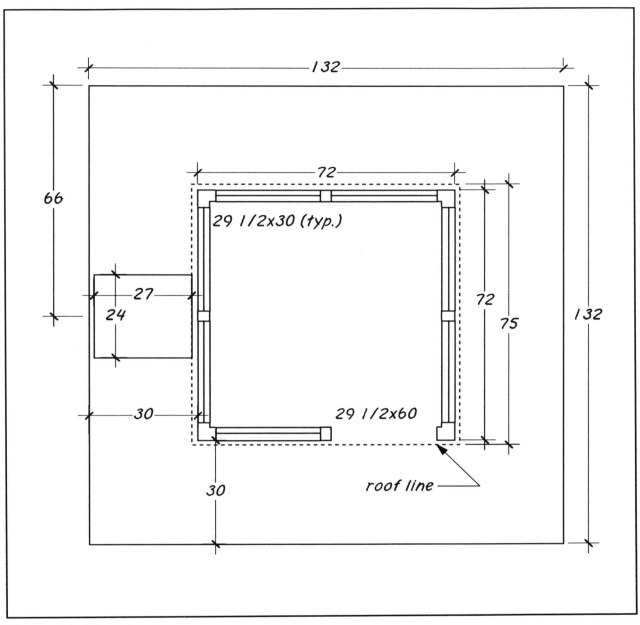

Figure 7.1. Plan view

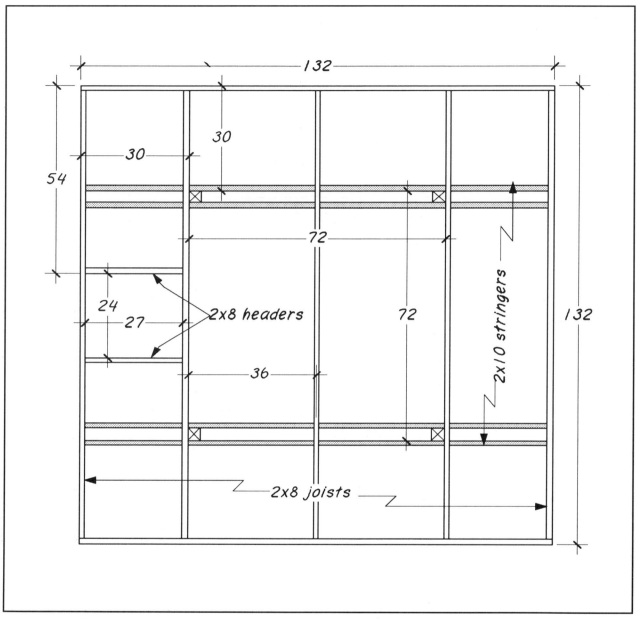

Figure 7.2. Post and joist plan

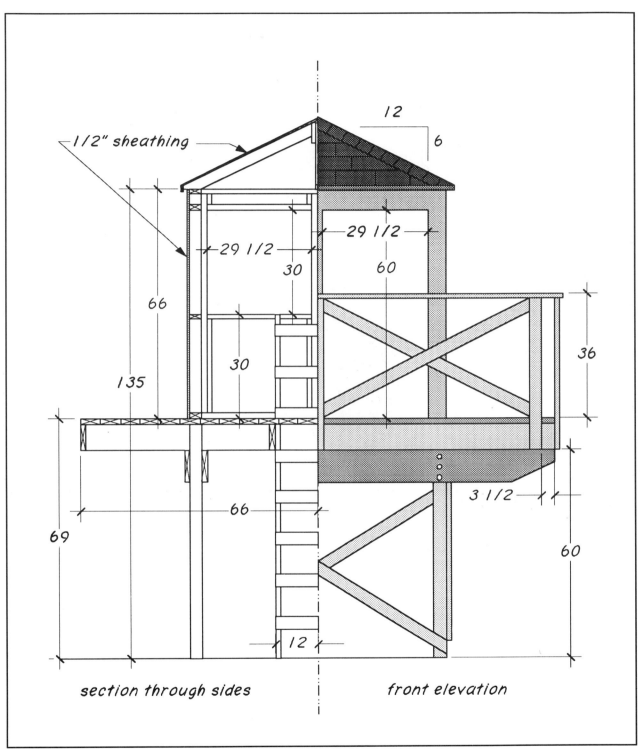

Figure 7.3. Section through sides and front elevation

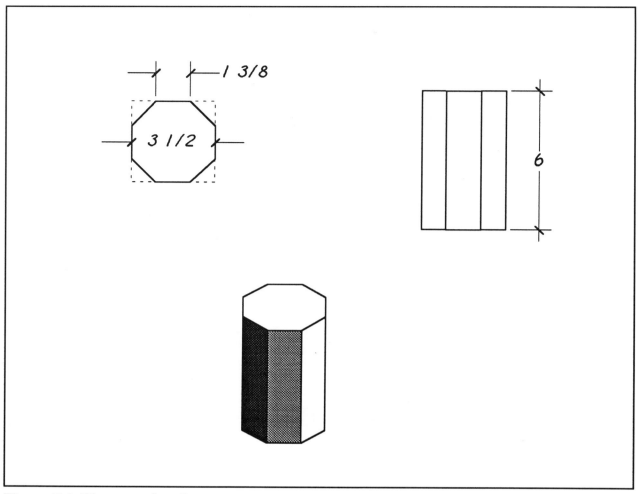

Figure 7.4. King post detail

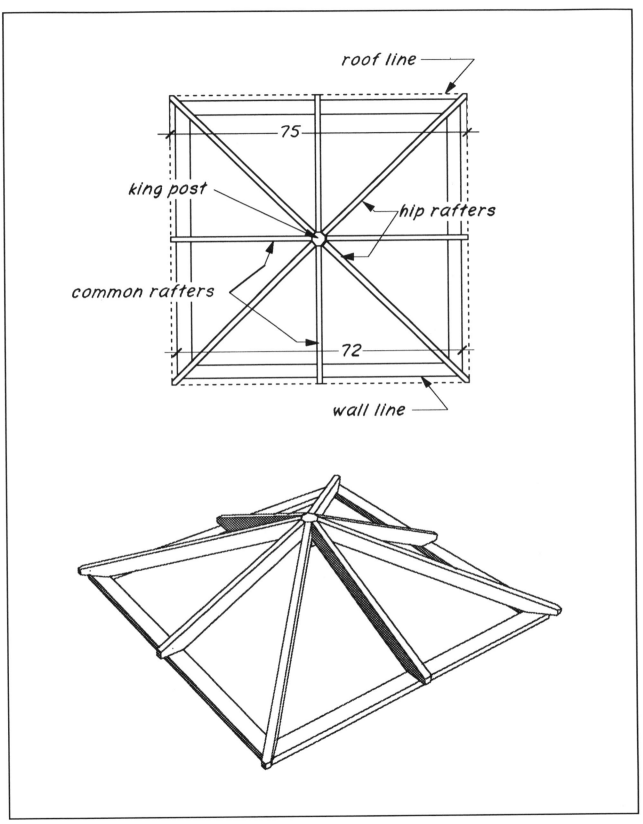

Figure 7.5. Roof detail

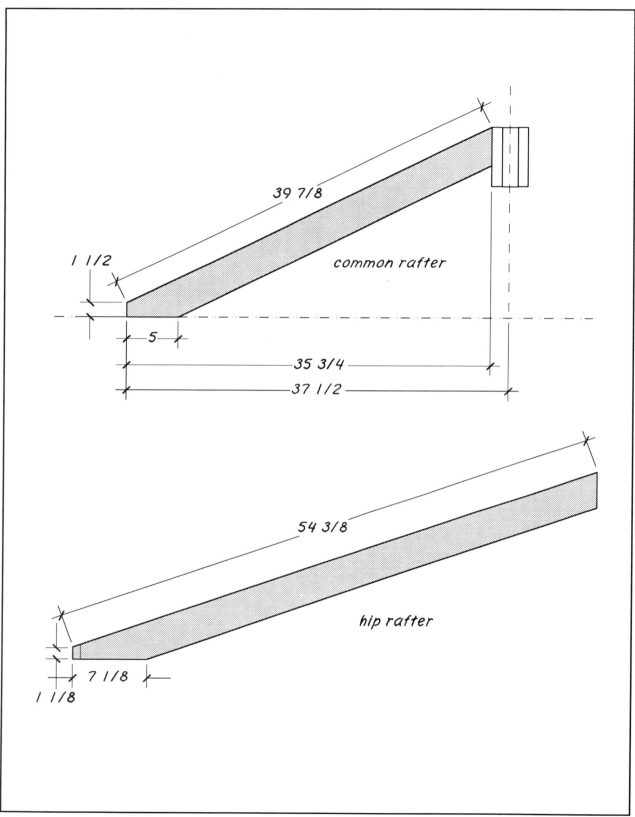

Figure 7.6. Rafter detail

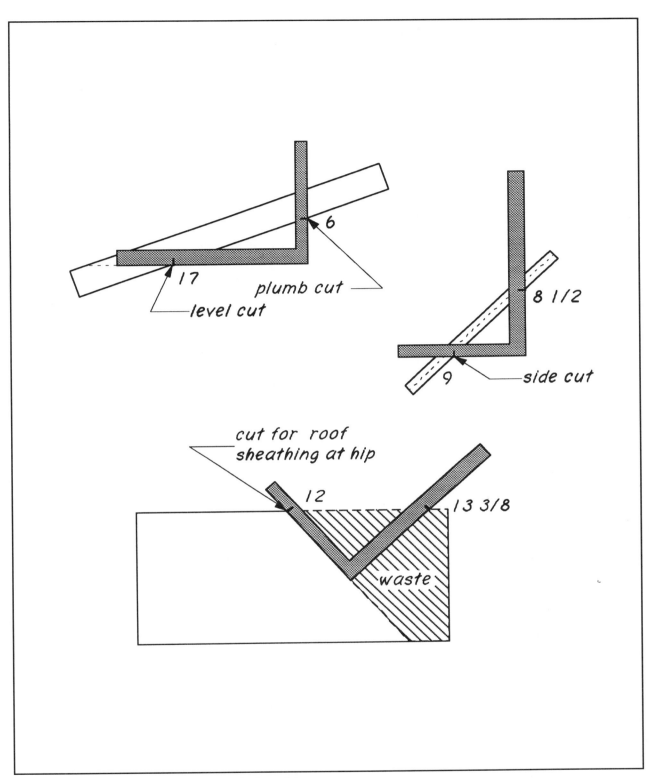

Figure 7.7. Cuts for hip rafter and sheathing

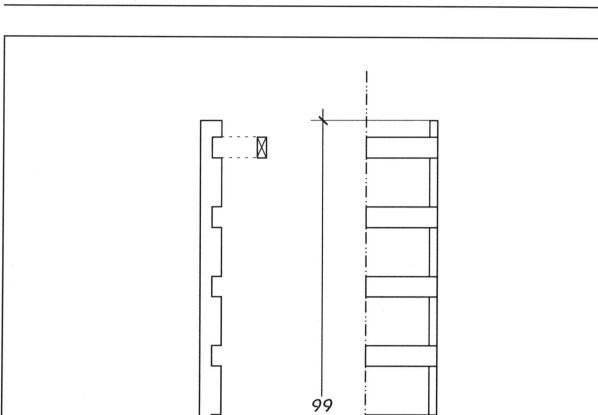

Figure 7.8. Ladder detail

· Project 8 ·

CLASSIC SWING SET

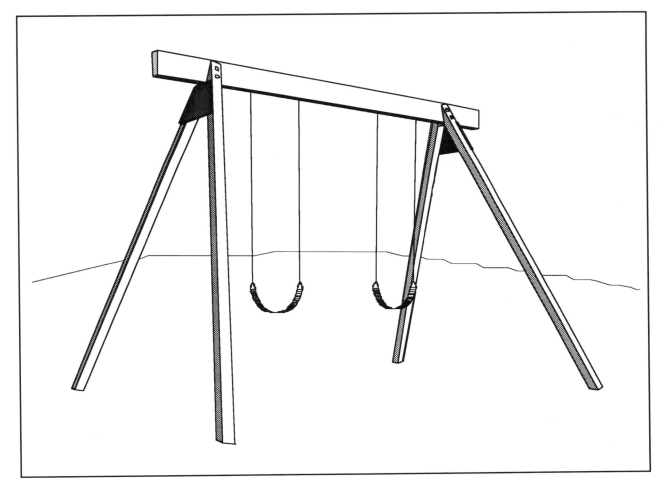

No doubt about it, kids love to swing. A backyard swing set is easy to build and relatively inexpensive, and it will keep the kids busy for hours.

All that's necessary for a swing is a sturdy place from which to hang it. The classic A-frame set featured here supports two swings, with plenty of room in between and to the sides for safety.

There are a number of ways to hang a swing and several kinds of hardware, from rope to chain, eyebolts to bearings, flexible rubber seat to a chunk of 2×6. Check your Yellow Pages under "Playground Equipment" for outlets of specialty hardware.

CUTTING AND ASSEMBLING THE LEGS

Before building the leg assemblies, stake out and dig the footings according to the dimensions shown in Figures 8.1 and 8.2.

Cut the legs from treated 4×4 fir, cedar, or redwood. The overall length of the legs allows the swing set to be embedded 12 inches below grade while yielding a clearance of 8 feet to the bottom of the beam. Figures 8.2 and 8.3 illustrate how the legs intersect the beam at a compound angle. Each angle is determined with the framing square, but only one cut is necessary. Make a 24-in-12 plumb cut at the top of each leg.

Lay out and bore $5/8$-inch-diameter holes for the $1/2$-inch bolts, as detailed in Figure 8.4. Use a chisel to create pockets in the legs so that the washers will fit flat and parallel to the beam.

Make two brace plates (Figure 8.3) out of $5/8$- or $3/4$-inch exterior grade plywood. Lay one pair of legs on a flat surface in the configuration shown in Figure 8.3. Space the legs apart at the top the width of the beam plus about $1/16$ inch (so that the beam will slip into place easily). Measure down the outside of each leg $80\frac{1}{2}$ inches. The distance between the two marks should be $75\frac{1}{2}$ inches. Temporarily nail a 2×4 or 1×4 across the legs at those points. Use screws or 8d galvanized nails and a generous amount of construction adhesive to secure the brace plate $7\frac{1}{2}$ inches below the top of the assembly. Space the nails 2 inches apart along the inside and outside edges of each leg. Build the other leg assembly in the same manner.

RAISING THE BEAM

Lay out the beam according to the dimensions given in Figure 8.2. Bore any necessary holes for mounting the equipment, but do not yet bore the holes for mounting the leg assemblies.

Using the framing square set at 24-in-6 (twice the incline of 24-in-12), lay out the angles on the beam at which to set the legs.

Place the leg assemblies on the ground, outside up and with the feet roughly over the holes in which they will fit. With the aid of an assistant, lift the peak of one of the leg assemblies, and bring one end of the beam into place. If necessary, prop the leg

Project 8 Materials List

Description	Quantity	Length in feet	Comments
4×8	1	14	Fir, cedar, or redwood beam
4×4	4	12	Pressure-treated fir, cedar, or redwood legs
Bolts with nuts and washers	2		$1/2" \times 6"$
Bolts with nuts and washers	2		$1\frac{1}{2}" \times 9"$
Brace plate	2		See text and Figure 8.2
Concrete mix	4		Sacks
Swing hardware			Specialty items—see text

assembly to help align it with the angle marks already drawn on the beam. Bore ⅝-inch-diameter holes through the beam, and bolt the legs to the beam. Now lift the opposite end of the beam, raising the other leg assembly into place at the same time.

Use caution, making certain that the beam is stable while aligning the leg assembly and boring the remaining holes.

Check that the beam is level in both directions at both ends. Pour about 8 inches of concrete around the base of each leg, sloping it away from the legs.

The surface of the concrete should be well below grade level so that it will not pose a hazard to children.

Install the swing hardware of your choice.

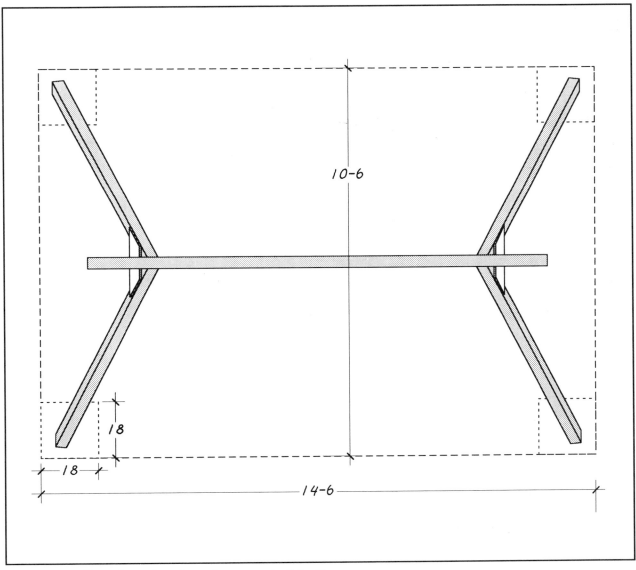

Figure 8.1. Top view showing placement of footings

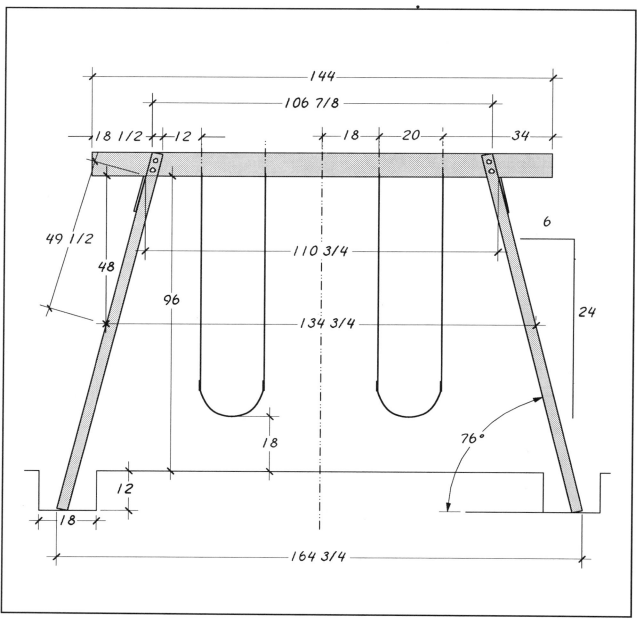

Figure 8.2. Front elevation

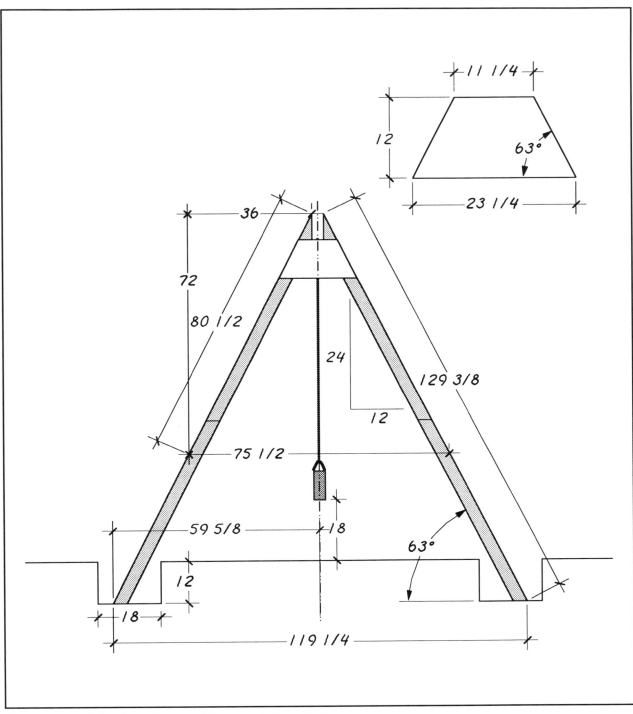

Figure 8.3. Side elevation and brace plate detail

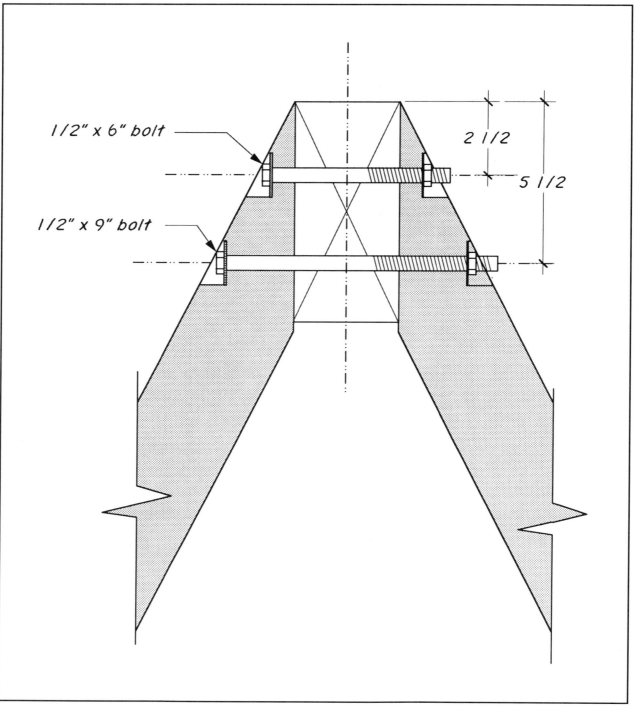

Figure 8.4. Bolt detail at beam

Project 9
HOMESTEAD

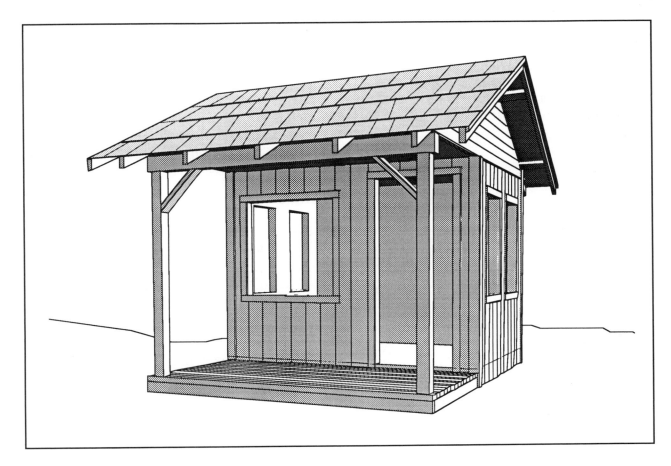

The Homestead is reminiscent of houses built on the plains during the days of the pioneers. Its 6-in-12, 26½-degree roof covers both the 48-square-foot house and the 32-square-foot front porch. The roof trusses bear on the back wall and the porch beam, leaving the front wall non-load bearing.

BUILDING THE FLOOR

Carefully study the plans and materials list before beginning. Consider ground slope and other conditions to determine special foundation needs.

From treated 2×6, cut two stringers 96 inches long and five joists 69 inches long.

Assemble the floor as described in part 1 and as shown in Figure 9.2.

Also install the porch stringer and joists. The stringer is 96 inches, and the joists are 45½ inches. All of the joists are placed 24 inches on center.

Let the porch posts at the front corners run wild, and trim them later. Be sure they are firmly braced until the trusses are secure.

BUILDING THE WALLS

Cut four plates 95 inches long for the front and back walls and four plates 64 inches long for the end walls. Tack the plates to the floor as described in part 1.

Lay out the door and window in the front wall using the dimensions shown in Figure 9.1. Each is built directly against the corner posts. Each end wall has a pair of 18×36 windows.

Count the number of studs you will need, and cut them 67½ inches long. Cut ten trimmers 58½ inches long and two (for the door) 64½ inches. Each of the headers is 3 inches longer than its rough opening is wide.

Because the roof load is carried by the back wall and the porch beam, none of the headers carry a load. Headers can be made of single or double 2×4s. Build the four posts for the front and back walls as described.

The floor is just big enough to allow you to build each wall one at a time. Build the back wall first. Separate the plates and lay them edge up on the floor. Nail in the corner posts and studs. Cut a doubler plate 88 inches long, and nail it to the top plate 3½ inches in from each end. Square the wall by measuring the diagonal dimensions. Do not include the doubler plate in the measure-

Project 9 Materials List

Description	Quantity	Length in feet	Comments
4×4	4	8	Pressure-treated posts
4×6	1	8	Porch beam
2×6	8	8	Pressure-treated stringers, joists, bridging
2×4	18	8	Pressure-treated porch componenets
2×4	10	8	Plates, misc.
2×4	5	10	Bottom chords
2×4	28	12	Studs, trimmers, misc.
2×4	7	14	Top chords, barge rafters
1×2	4	8	Cedar rake mold
Pier blocks	14		
¾" flooring	2		Sheets, treated
½" sheathing	11		Sheets
Nails, screws			As needed
Post caps	2		

ments. If necessary, tack the wall to the floor to keep it in place. Nail on the sheathing using 7d or 8d nails (galvanized if you will not be applying siding later), spaced 8 to 10 inches.

Set the back wall aside and build the front wall. Face-nail the corners, studs, and king studs into place. Nail the trimmers to the bottom plate and to their king studs. Nail in the headers, sills, and cripples, using 8d toe nails where necessary. Cut a doubler plate 88 inches long, and nail it to the top plate. Square the wall and sheath it. Do not cut the bottom plate in the door opening until the wall is nailed to the floor.

Build the side walls, but do not nail on the 71-inch doubler plates or any sheathing until later.

Set the front and back walls in place on the floor, and anchor them with 16d nails driven into the joists and stringers every 16 to 24 inches. Then set the end walls into place and nail them down. True up the corners, temporarily bracing the end walls, and nail them together. Nail on the doubler plates to tie the walls together.

Next, using a long straightedge, level over from the top of the front wall to the porch posts. From these marks measure down 5½ inches (the thickness of the porch beam), and cut the posts. Cut the beam 96 inches long and install two post caps. Install the beam, leaving the ends hanging 1½ inches beyond each post.

Cut a length of 2×4 19 inches long and with 45-degree angles at each end (Figure 9.3) for the braces under the beam. Nail the braces in place with 8d galvanized finish nails.

Finally, sheath the side walls.

BUILDING THE ROOF

Refer to Figure 9.5 for the lengths of the top and bottom chords. The cut for the bottom chords is a level cut—that is, the line is marked against the body of the framing square set at 6-in-12. The three trusses that span the floor have a center strut, and the gable trusses have extra struts to carry the sheathing and siding.

Lay out each truss on a smooth, solid surface. Nail the gussets into place with 4d galvanized nails or 1½-inch roofing nails about 2 inches apart. For added strength, apply a bead of construction adhesive. Flip the truss, and nail the gussets on the other side. Do not use gussets on the outside of the gable trusses, as they will interfere with the sheathing.

Lay out the trusses 24 inches on center. Also lay out a long 2×4 or 1×4 to temporarily hold the trusses in place along the peak. Toe-nail the first gable truss to the plate with 8d nails, and brace it securely. Install the rest of the trusses.

The gable overhang is 12 inches, and each barge rafter is held in place with a pair of out hangers (see part 1, Figure 19). The barge rafters are the same length as the top chords of the trusses. After nailing on the sheathing, install the rake molding at the gable ends.

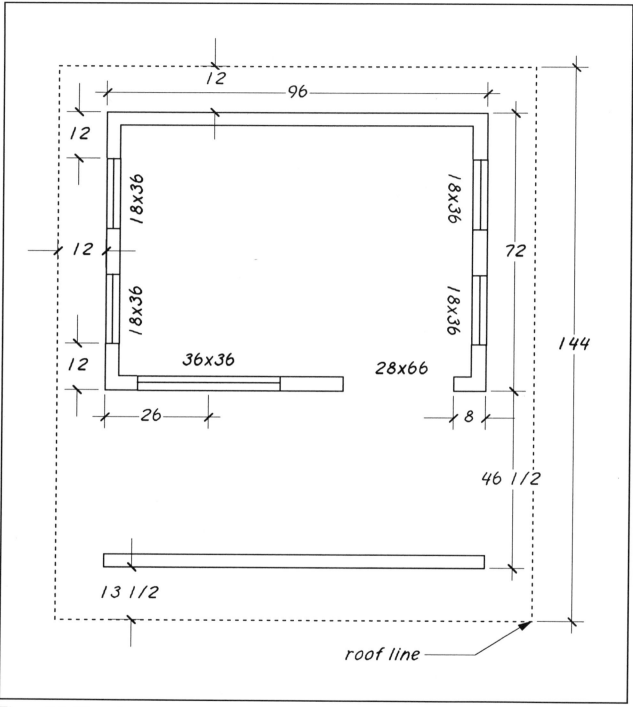

Figure 9.1. Plan view

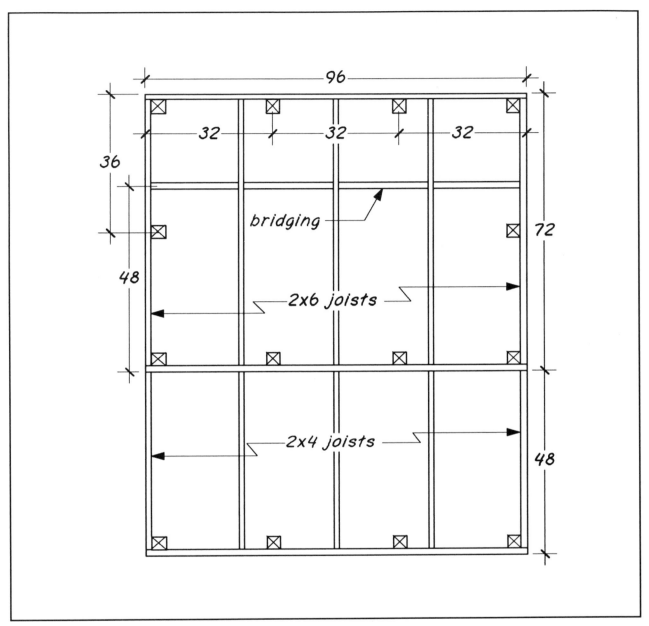

Figure 9.2. Foundation plan

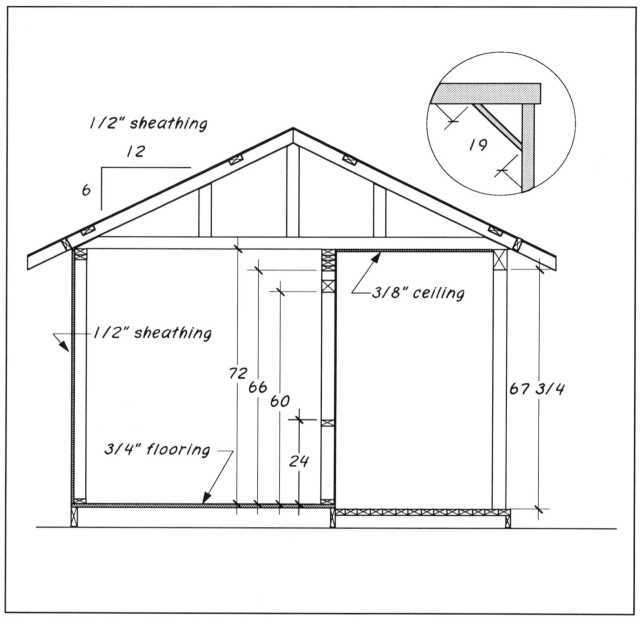

Figure 9.3. Section with inset showing brace at porch

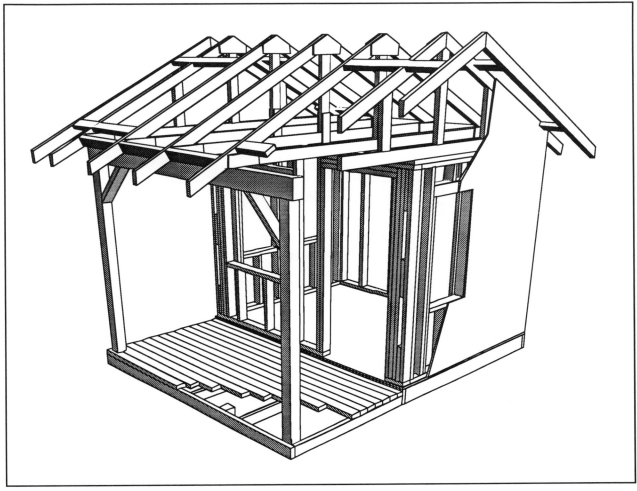

Figure 9.4. Framing plan

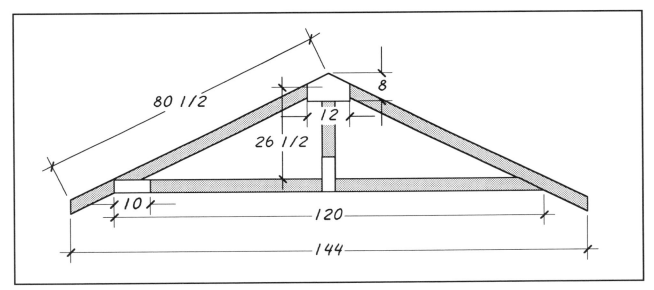

Figure 9.5. Truss detail

▪ Project 10 ▪
MODULAR CLIMB-AROUND

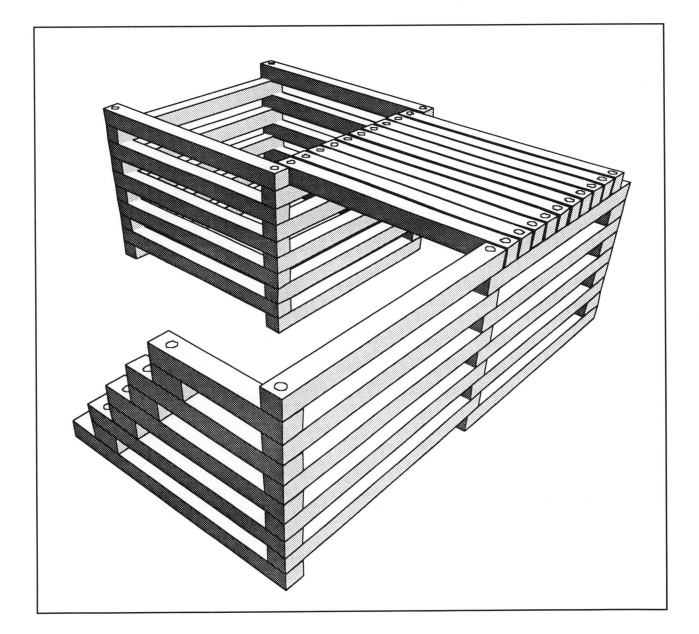

The Modular Climb-Around is the simplest structure presented here. It's also the most versatile. The basic components are treated 48-inch-long 4×4s. Any number of them can be bolted together in a variety of configurations with lengths of threaded rod and carriage bolts.

The structure illustrated here uses forty-five pieces, with four of them progressively shorter by 6 inches, and eight 6-inch spacers. This piece of play equipment should be installed on level ground. For safety, cover the area with 6 to 10 inches of resilient material, such as bark chips.

ASSEMBLING THE BOX SECTION

Begin by assembling the box section. Select twenty pieces, and lay out the bore points on each end (Figure 10.3). Bore 5/8-inch-diameter holes through each end of all but the uppermost pieces. In these, counterbore a pair of 1 1/2-inch-diameter holes about 1 1/2 inches deep. Finish the bore with 5/8-inch-diameter bit (inset, Figure 10.3). Take care that the holes are perpendicular and accurately placed.

Before assembling the box section, you will need to bore and counterbore the piece that will support the bridge, because the counterbores are on the underside of the piece. Although this step isn't absolutely necessary, counterboring the underside of the supporting piece will allow you to recess both ends of the bolts that secure the bridge. While you're at it, repeat the layout and borings on the supporting piece that will fit in the wall section, which you'll assemble later.

Select one piece to use as the bridge support. Lay out the bridge sections, and perform the above bore-counterbore operation on the *underside* of the support. (To save time, do the opposite bridge support while you're at it.)

To continue the box assembly, take four 36-inch lengths of threaded rod, and fit one end with a washer and hex nut. This will be the top end of the rod, so turn the nut down just far enough to cover the end. Slip a rod through the upper face of each of the top 4×4s. Put the 4×4s upside down on the ground with the rods sticking up. Be careful not to lean over and poke yourself in the face!

Slip the remainder of the 4×4s over the rods, and put on the washers and nuts. Lay the assembly on one side, and tighten the nuts in rotation (a little at a time for each one), checking for square as you go. Don't cut off the ends of the rods—they will keep the unit from sliding. Upend the assembly and put it in position.

ASSEMBLING THE WALL SECTION AND BRIDGE

You will assemble the wall section, including the stepped portion, flat on the ground. For the wall you will need eleven pieces 48 inches long and eight pieces 6 inches long. You also will need one each 42 inches, 36

Project 10 Materials List

Description	Quantity	Length in feet	Comments
4×4	23	8	Pressure-treated fir
Threaded rod	11	3	1/2"
Hex nuts	62		1/2"
Washers	62		1/2"

inches, 30 inches, and 24 inches long. For the bridge, you will need ten pieces 48 inches long.

Lay out and bore all the holes and counterbores, including the underside of the bridge support, if not already done. Lay the pieces on the ground and bolt them together. You will need three pieces of threaded rod 36 inches long and four pieces 6 inches long. Swing the stepped portion up and tighten it, making sure it is square.

Lift the wall and position it relative to the box.

Bore the necessary holes in the bridge pieces, and bolt them in place with 5-inch lengths of threaded rod. (You can also use 5-inch bolts.)

Plug the holes with pieces of 1½-inch-diameter dowel. Tap a length of dowel into a hole, then cut it off. Use a power sander to bring the plug flush with the surface.

Note: If the wood is wet during assembly, the joints will loosen as the wood dries out. In this case, wait for a period of hot, dry weather and retighten the bolts before plugging the holes.

To anchor the stepped section, bore a ½-inch hole through the end, and drive a 24-inch length of rod (or rebar) through the hole and into the ground.

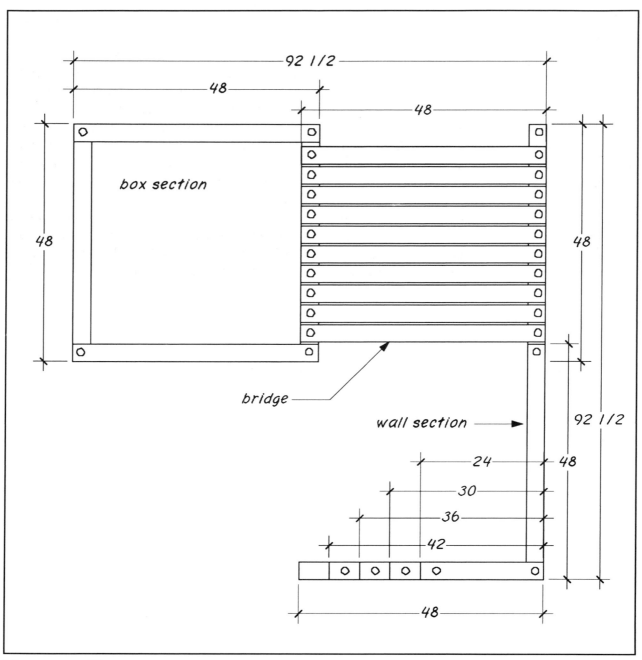

Figure 10.1. Plan view

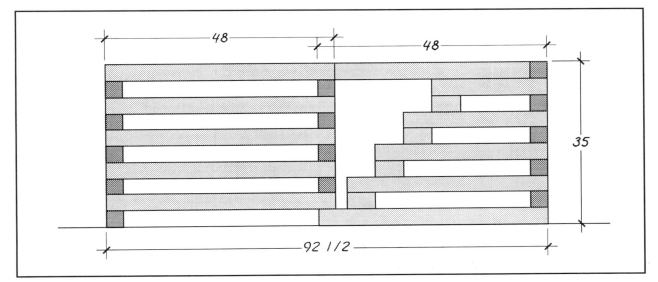

Figure 10.2. Side elevation

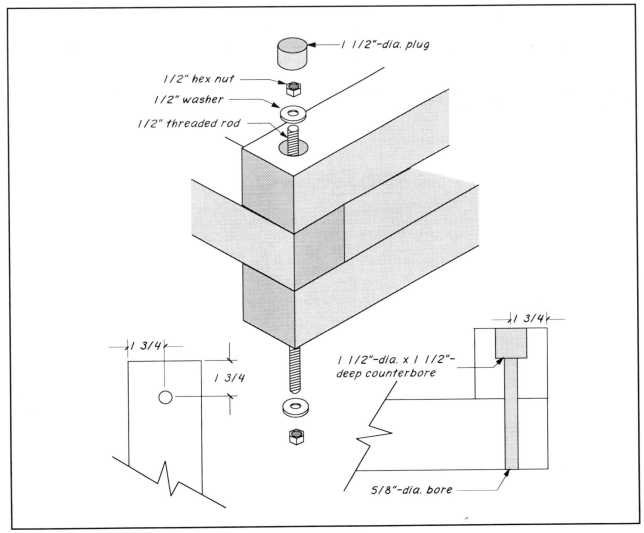

Figure 10.3. Corner joint detail

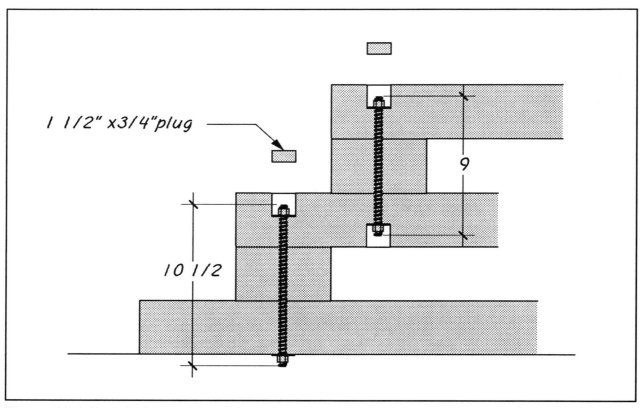

Figure 10.4. Detail of stepped-portion of wall

▪ Project 11 ▪
CLASSIC GAMBREL BARN

Project 11 Materials List

Description	Quantity	Length in feet	Comments
4 × 4	2	8	Pressure-treated posts
2 × 6	4	12	Pressure-treated stringers, bridging
2 × 4	15	8	Short studs, trimmers, misc.
2 × 4	25	12	Plates, truss chords, studs, headers
1 × 6	2	12	Cedar rake mold
Pier blocks	8		
¾" flooring	2		Sheets, treated
½" sheathing	7		Sheets
Nails, screws			As needed

Barns come in all shapes and sizes, and their function is strictly utilitarian. Yet there is something aesthetically pleasing about the classic lines of the gambrel roof. The gambrel roof of the playhouse illustrated here covers 66 square feet. The playhouse has a wide front door and plenty of window area.

BUILDING THE FLOOR
Carefully study the plans and materials list before beginning. Consider ground slope and other conditions to determine special foundation needs.

The floor is a simple 72-inch square with no porch. From treated 2 × 6, cut two stringers 72 inches long and four joists 69 inches long. Assemble the floor as described in part 1 and as shown in Figure 11.2.

BUILDING THE WALLS
Because you will need a flat, solid surface on which to build the trusses, consider making them first, before you start the walls.

When you begin the walls, build the short side walls first. You will fill in the end walls after the roof trusses are up. Cut six plates 71 inches long. Tack two plates for each wall to the floor, as described in part 1.

Lay out the studs, centering the 36 × 18 windows in the walls. The studs are 45 inches long, and the trimmers are 41½ inches long. Each header is 39 inches long and should be 4 × 4, either solid or built up. The sills are 36 inches long. Nail the walls together with a corner post at each end. Then nail on the top plate.

Square the wall by measuring the diagonal dimensions. If necessary, tack the wall to the floor to keep it in place. Nail on the sheathing using 7d or 8d nails (galvanized if no siding will be applied later) spaced 8 inches apart. Nail each wall in place on the floor, and brace it solidly before proceeding. Make sure the walls are plumb. Also check that the measurement across the top of each wall is the same as across the bottom.

BUILDING THE ROOF
The gambrel roof is made of trusses with a dual pitch. Figure 11.5 gives the chord lengths and gusset dimensions. Figure 11.6 gives the cuts for the framing square. Notice that even though the rises of the upper and

lower chords are different, the same setting of the square (20¾-in-12) will give the correct plumb and level cuts for each.

Lay out each truss on a smooth, solid surface. Secure the gussets into place with 4d galvanized nails or 1½-inch roofing nails spaced about 2 inches apart in all directions. For added strength, apply a bead of construction adhesive. Flip the truss and nail the gussets on the other side. Do not use gussets on the outside of the gable trusses, as they will interfere with the sheathing.

Lay out the trusses 24 inches on center. Also lay out a long 2×4 or 1×4 to temporarily hold the trusses in place along the peak. Toe-nail the first gable truss to the plate with 8d nails; brace it securely. Install the rest of the trusses. Nail in the bird blocks.

Once the trusses are in place, nail down and lay out the bottom plate for the front and back walls, centering the door and window openings.

Hold each stud in plumb against the gable truss and mark the angle, nailing each stud in place as you go. Nail the trimmers to the king studs, and install the headers and sills for the windows. If you plan to install a ceiling, install backing along the inside of each gable.

Next, nail the sheathing to the front and back walls.

The 2×4 barge rafters are the same lengths as the truss chords and are nailed directly to the sheathing. Once they are in place, nail on the roof sheathing. Use 1×6 cedar for the rake mold, keeping it flush with the upper edge of the sheathing.

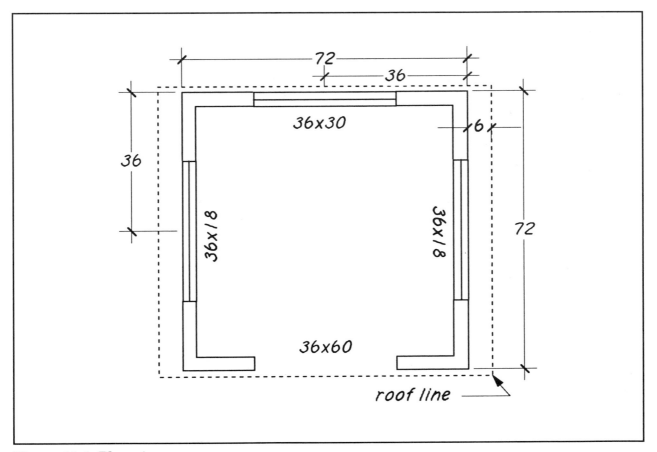

Figure 11.1. Plan view

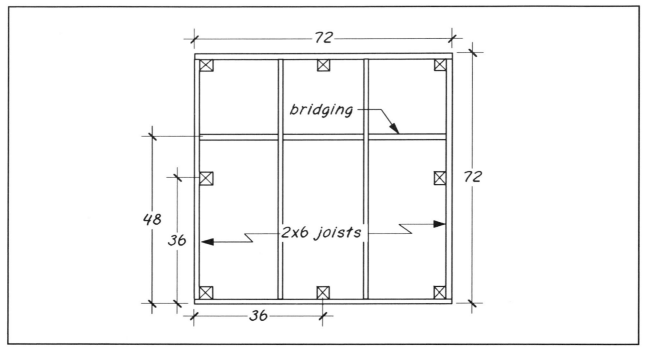

Figure 11.2. Foundation plan

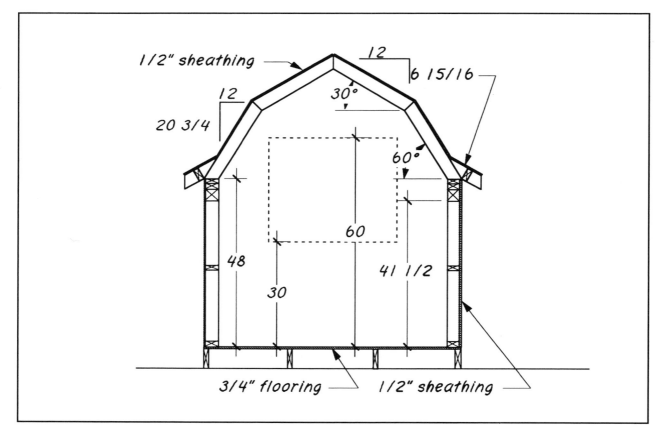

Figure 11.3. Section

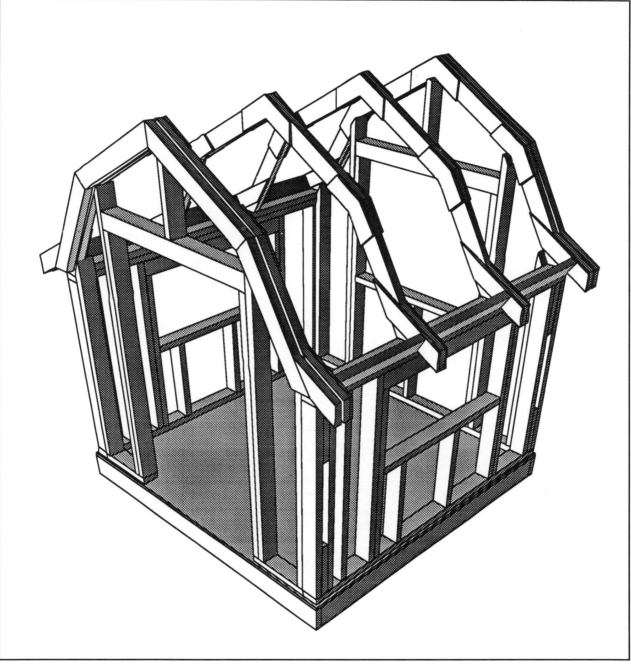

Figure 11.4. Framing plan

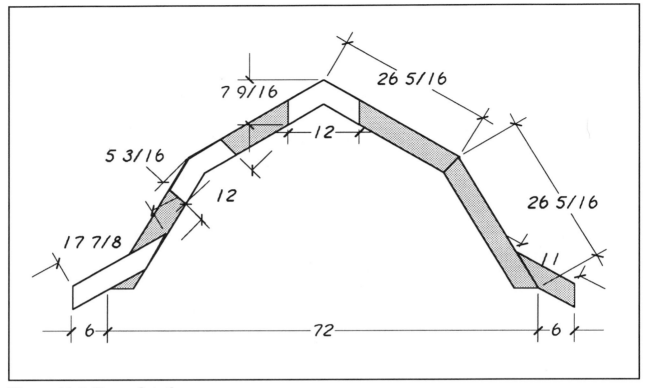

Figure 11.5. Truss detail

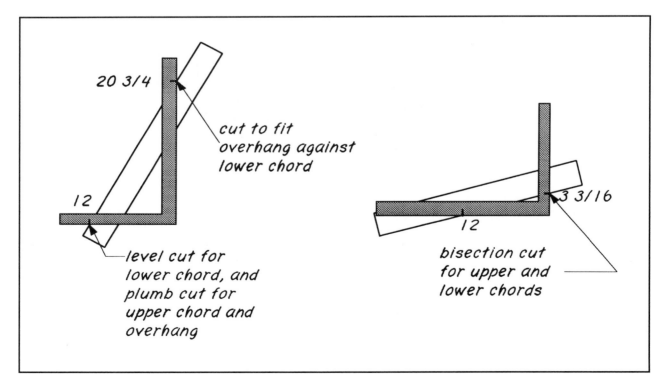

Figure 11.6. Cuts for truss chords

▪ Project 12 ▪

SWING-BAR COMBO

Project 12 Materials List

Description	Quantity	Length in feet	Comments
4 × 4	4	12	Pressure-treated posts
4 × 4	1	14	Pressure-treated posts
4 × 6	4	8	Beam
Bolts with nut and washers	4		½" × 11½"
Bolts with nut and washers	4		½" × 9"
Pipe	1	6	¾" (inside diameter) galvanized
Floor flange	4		¾" galvanized
Flathead wood screws	16		#12 × 1¼"
Swing hardware			See text
Concrete mix	6		Sacks

This project incorporates a single swing and a pair of bars, each at a different height.

ASSEMBLING AND SETTING THE POSTS

Lay out and dig the holes according to the dimensions shown in Figure 12.1. Cut the long posts so that their tops will be approximately 10 feet, 6 inches from the highest point of the ground.

Bore ⅝-inch-diameter holes in the posts and beam as shown in Figure 12.2 and the spacers as shown in Figure 12.3. Take all measurements from the top. Also bore the necessary holes for the swing hardware (Figure 12.1).

Bolt the pieces together, then nail a 2 × 4 or 1 × 4 across the posts at a point just above ground level to keep the bottoms properly spaced. Raise the assembly and brace it securely, ensuring that the posts are plumb and the beam is level.

Brace the short posts in place, taking care to keep them in line with the inside faces of the main posts.

Pour concrete mix around the posts. The concrete should slope away from the posts, with the top well below grade level to avoid creating a potential hazard for children. Wait at least twenty-four hours before removing the braces.

INSTALLING THE HARDWARE

There are a number of ways to hang a swing and several kinds of hardware, from rope to chain, eyebolts to bearings, flexible rubber seat to a chunk of 2 × 6. Check your Yellow Pages under "Playground Equipment" for local outlets of specialty hardware.

The bars are lengths of ¾-inch pipe secured to the posts with galvanized floor flanges. Not everyone has in his toolbox the items necessary to cut and thread galvanized pipe, so it's likely you'll have to take the pipe somewhere to have this work done. Many lumberyards keep pipe-fitting equipment on hand and will do the work for little or no charge. Any sheet metal or plumbing shop also can do the work.

Measure the distance between the main uprights and the short posts (it should be

$32\frac{1}{2}$ inches). Cut the pipe about $\frac{3}{8}$ inch shorter than this distance. Thread a flange to each end of the pipe, and adjust them so that the overall length matches the distance between the posts. Use #12 × 1¼-inch flat-

head screws to secure the flanges to the posts.

Spread 6 to 10 inches of resilient material, such as bark chips, around the play area.

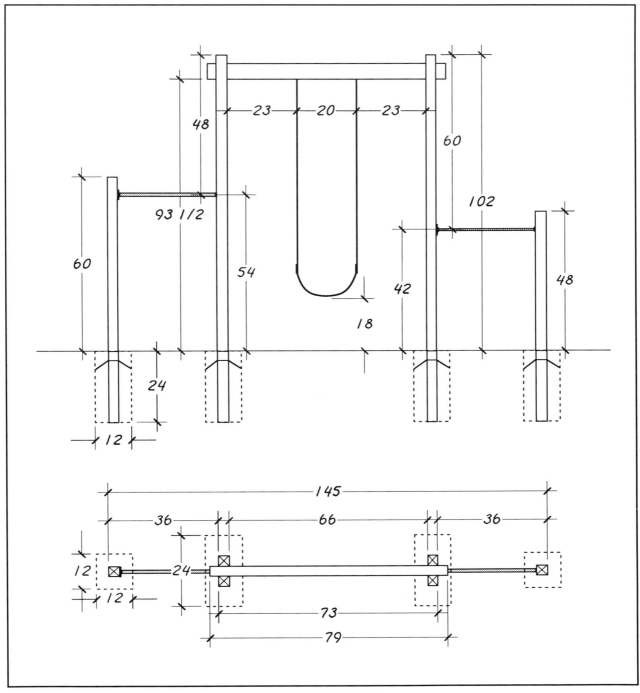

Figure 12.1. Front elevation and plan view

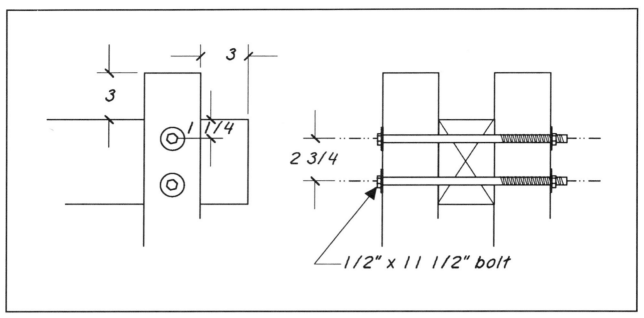

Figure 12.2. Bolt detail at beam

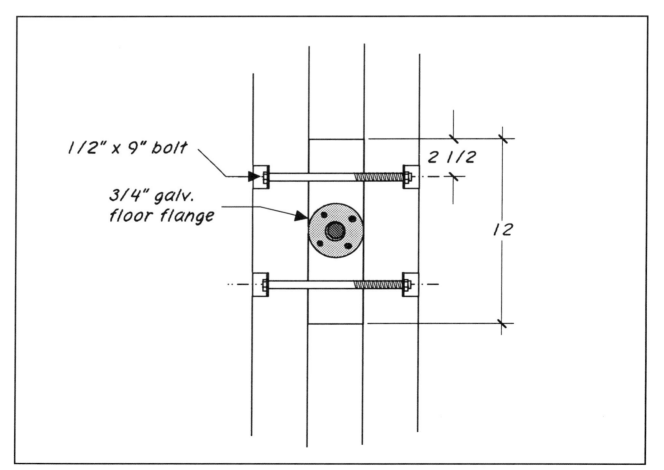

Figure 12.3. Bolt detail at spacer also showing floor flange. (See also Figure 14.4.)

▪ Project 13 ▪
STILT HOUSE

The Stilt House is nearly 6 feet off the ground. The house portion covers half the 96-square-foot deck. It has a 2-in-12, 9½-degree shed roof with a 12-inch reversed overhang along the front.

BUILDING THE SUPPORTING STRUCTURE AND DECK

The supporting structure consists of the posts and their braces, 2 × 10 stringers, 2 × 8 joists, and 2 × 6 decking.

Refer to Figure 13.1 for post locations. For best results, use batter boards to lay out the posts, as described in part 1. Set the posts in holes 24 to 30 inches deep. Use temporary braces to hold the posts in place while checking the dimensions. When the posts are plumb, parallel, and square, fill the holes with concrete. Do not pile the concrete higher than grade level, as it may present a hazard to children. Pour a 24 × 30-inch concrete pad as a base for the ladder. Allow at least twenty-four hours for the concrete to set before removing the braces.

After the concrete has set up, trim the posts. Begin with the post at the highest point on the ground, marking it at 5 feet above grade. Level over from that point to each of the other posts, and cut them at that height.

The next step is to bolt the 2 × 10 stringers to the posts. Use three ½ × 8½-inch bolts with washers at each post. Center the bolts on the posts and approximately 1¼ inches in from the top and bottom edges of the stringers (Figure 13.4). The stringers are 8 feet long and chamfered at each end (Figure 13.4). Lay out the posts, and mark the locations of the bolts on the stringers. Tack blocks to the posts on which to rest the stringers. Set the stringers on the blocks, and use one or two nails to hold them in place while you bore the ⅝-inch-diameter holes and install the bolts. When the stringers are bolted in place, nail on the braces with 16d galvanized nails.

Install the deck system. Cut four joists 11 feet, 9 inches long. Toe-nail the outer joists to the 2 × 10 stringers. Face nail the 2 × 8 end stringers to the joists using 16d galvanized nails. Set the two intermediate joists as shown. Next, form the ladder opening with 2 × 8s.

Working from one end to the other, install the 2 × 6 decking using 16d galvanized nails or deck screws. Space the boards about the thickness of a nail. As you progress, check the remaining distance at each end to ensure that the boards are running even and you won't end up with a narrow space to fill. (Over a long span, you can adjust the spacing in order to end up with a full 2 × 6, 2 × 4, or 2 × 2, so that no ripping will be necessary.)

BUILDING THE WALLS

To allow for the sheathing, the inside edges of the walls are set 4 inches in from the perimeter. Cut four plates 95 inches long for the front and back walls and four 64 inches long for the end walls. Lay out the openings as shown in Figure 13.2.

Cut the studs for the front wall 67½ inches. The door trimmers are 64½ inches, and the header is 31 inches. The window trimmers are 58½ inches, and the header is 39 inches. The studs for the back and end walls are 56⅛ inches, and the headers are also 39 inches. Nail together two corner posts for the back wall and two for the front wall.

Build the back wall first. The doubler plate is 88 inches long. Square the wall and sheath it (if preferred) before nailing it in place on the floor. Don't include the doubler plate during the squaring procedure. Brace it securely before building the end walls.

Notice in Figure 13.3 that the end-wall doubler plates lap the back wall but not the front. They are 60½ inches. Wait until the gable rafters and studs are in place before installing any sheathing on the end walls.

Project 13 Materials List

Description	Quantity	Length in feet	Comments
4×4	6	8	Pressure-treated posts
2×10	6	8	Cedar stringers
2×8	3	8	Cedar stringers, headers
2×8	4	12	Cedar joists
2×6	26	8	Treated or cedar decking
2×4	22	8	Rafters, braces, plates, misc.
2×4	20	10	Studs, braces, misc.
2×4	15	12	Studs, plates, misc.
2×2	21	8	Cedar balusters
1×2	3	8	Cedar rake mold
$\frac{1}{2}$" sheathing	9		Sheets
Nails, screws			As needed
Concrete mix	6		Sacks
Bolts with nuts and washers	12		$\frac{1}{2}" \times 8\frac{1}{2}"$

Build the front wall, and raise it against the end walls. Check that all corners are plumb; nail the corners together. Sheath the front wall before beginning the roof.

BUILDING THE ROOF

Cut five rafters and two barge rafters to the specifications shown in Figure 13.5. They are the same length, but the barge rafters have no seat cuts. Also cut fourteen short rafters and ten plywood gussets.

Nail the main rafters in place. Then glue (with construction adhesive) and nail the gussets to the short rafters. Slip the short rafters into place, having first applied a bead of glue to each main rafter, and nail the gussets to the main rafters.

Next, sheath the end walls. Then nail lengths of 2×2 along the rake on both ends. To these 2×2 spacers, nail the barge rafters.

Nail bird blocks between the rafters and, if you plan to install a ceiling, the necessary backing. Finally, sheath the roof, and finish the gables with rake molding.

BUILDING THE LADDER AND BALUSTRADE

Install siding and trim before installing the ladder.

Build the ladder according to the dimensions given in Figure 13.6, notching the uprights to receive the 2×4 rungs. Cut the rungs slightly shorter than the width of the deck opening to ensure an easy fit. To make the notches, clamp the uprights together and lay out the rungs. Set your circular saw to $1\frac{1}{2}$ inches and make passes about $\frac{1}{4}$ inch apart through each location. Separate the uprights, and knock out the waste with a hammer. Clean up the notches with a chisel. Use screws to fasten the rungs to the uprights. Put the ladder in place in the deck opening, and screw the uprights to the headers.

Cut the balusters 45 inches long and bevel the tops. Use screws or 16d galvanized nails to mount them to the deck. Space them 6 inches on center. Install the 2×4 rails onto the balusters as shown in Figures 13.3 and 13.4.

The ladder is positioned in such a way that the opening in the deck can easily be cordoned off with a length of rope or chain. Alternatively, install a hinged trapdoor.

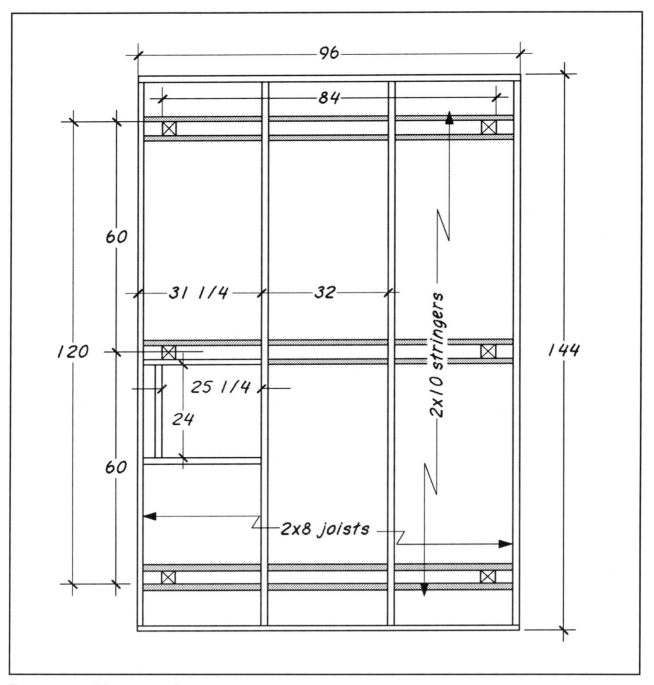

Figure 13.1. Plan view of supporting structure

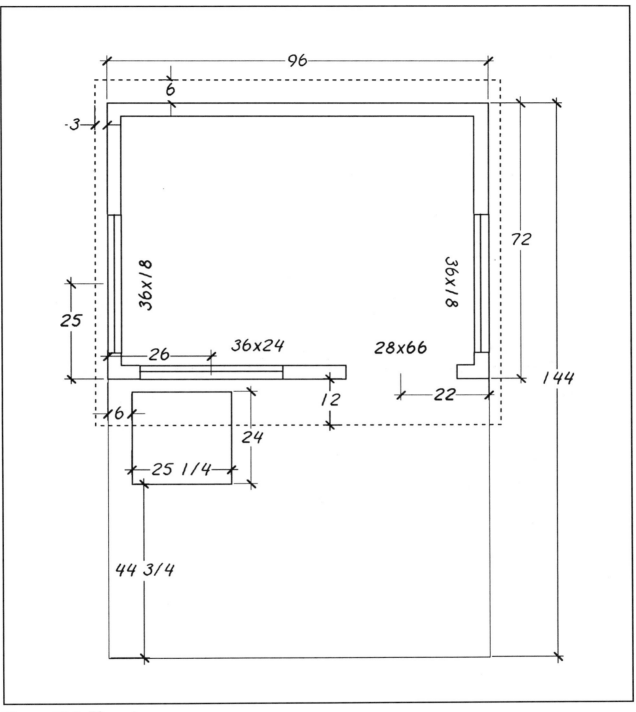

Figure 13.2. Plan view

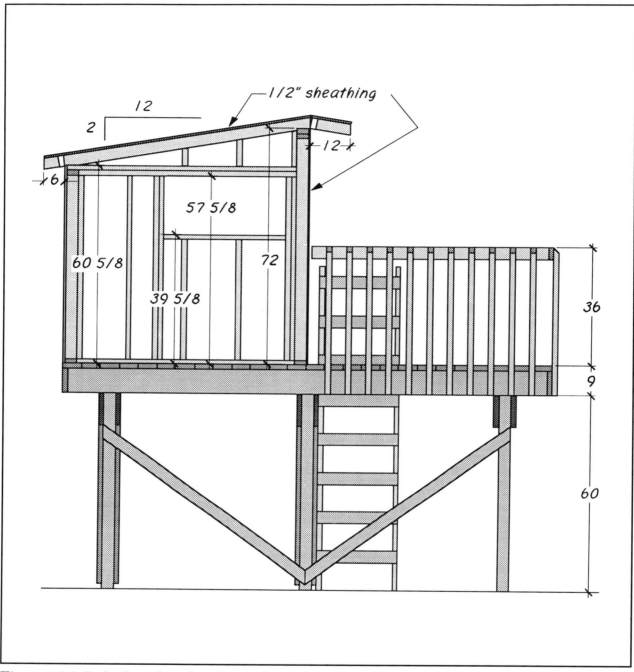

Figure 13.3. Left elevation showing wall frame and balustrade

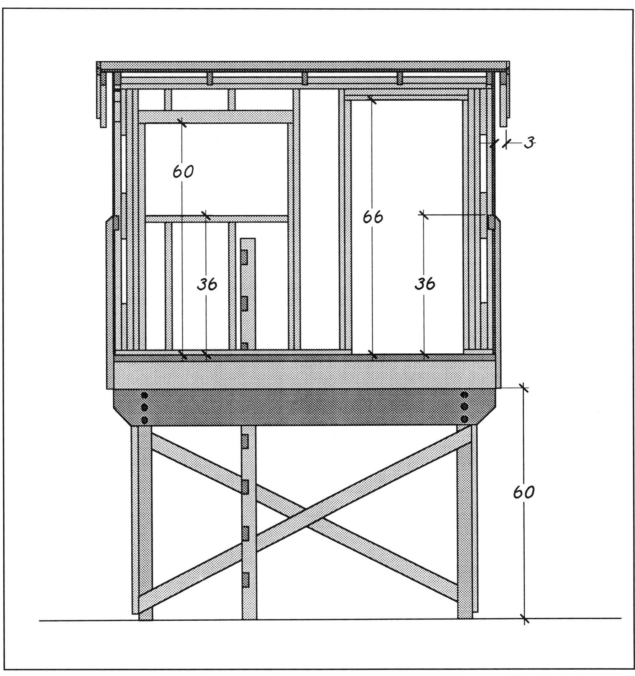

Figure 13.4. Front elevation showing wall frame (front balustrade removed for clarity)

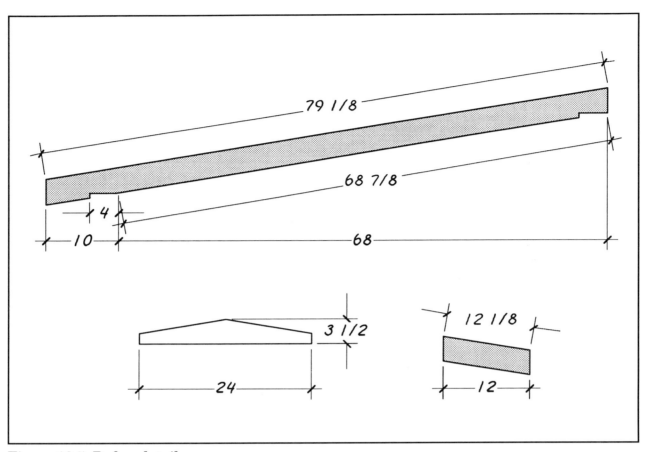

Figure 13.5. Rafter detail

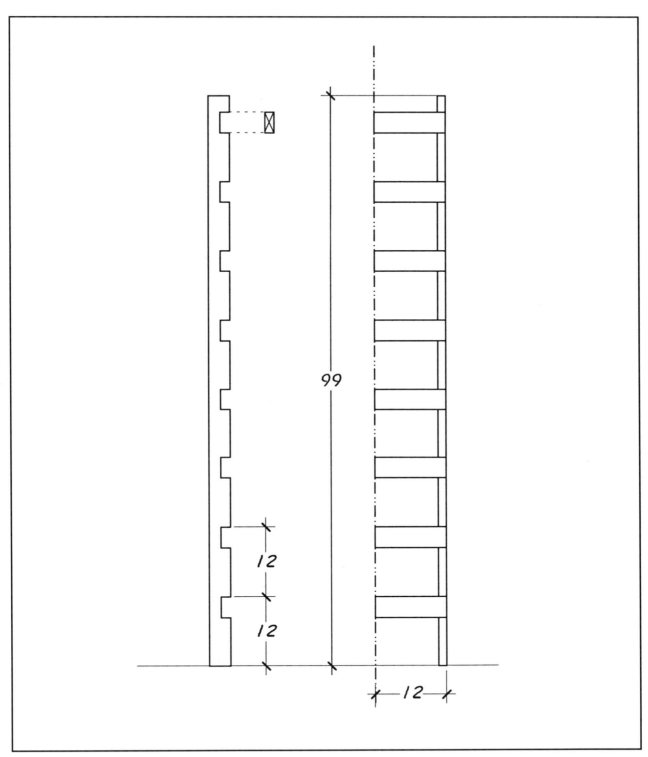

Figure 13.6. Ladder detail

▪ Project 14 ▪

MONKEY TOWER

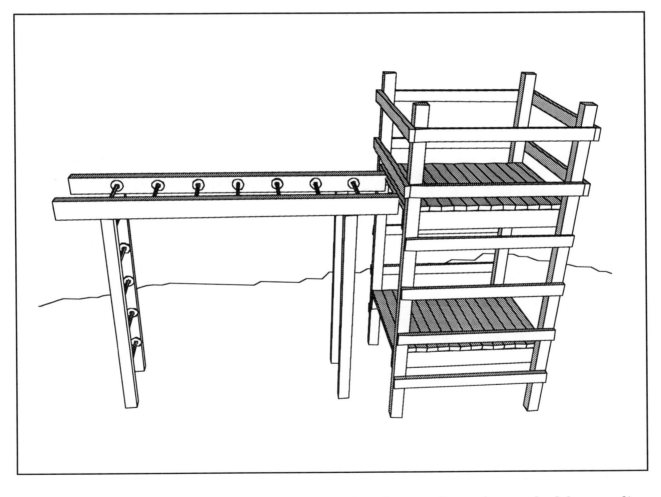

The Monkey Tower is combination of two components: the tower itself and a monkey bar system. The tower has two levels. The first is open on two sides and serves as a takeoff platform for the monkey bars. The upper tier is at the same level as the mon-

key bars and can be reached by crawling across the bars or climbing up and over the tower sides. The tower's rails are wide enough apart that a child can fit between them but not so far apart that they are difficult to master. The tower is assembled

Project 14 Materials List

Description	Quantity	Length in feet	Comments
4 × 4	4	12	Pressure-treated posts
4 × 4	4	8	Pressure-treated posts
4 × 6	2	8	Cedar or redwood beam
2 × 6	2	8	Cedar stringer
2 × 4	20	8	Cedar rail, decking
2 × 4	2	10	
Post cap	4		
Pipe	1	20	¾" (inside diameter) galvanized
Floor flange	24		¾" galvanized
Flathead wood screws	96		#12 × 1¼"
Deck screws			As needed
Concrete mix	8		Sacks

with 3½-inch deck screws. The monkey bars' beams are secured with post caps. The ¾-inch galvanized pipe bars are threaded into galvanized floor flanges, which in turn are secured to the posts and beams with #12 × 1¼-inch flathead screws.

SETTING THE POSTS

Lay out the posts according to the measurements shown in Figure 14-1. Dig the holes approximately 12 inches across and 24 inches deep. Set the posts in the holes and brace them securely. Then mix and pour in the concrete, sloping it away from the posts. Make sure it is 3 or 4 inches below grade. Let the concrete cure for at least twenty-four hours before removing the braces.

BUILDING THE TOWER

Begin by mounting the 2 × 6 stringers at the elevations shown in Figure 14.3, then install the decking. Install the rails, and cut the tops of the tower posts even.

BUILDING THE MONKEY BARS

Cut the tops of the monkey bars posts at 66½ inches, then nail a post cap onto each one. Next, secure the beams in place.

The bars are lengths of ¾-inch pipe threaded on each end and secured to the post-and-beam assemblies with galvanized floor flanges. Many lumberyards keep pipe-fitting equipment on hand and will do the cutting and threading for little or no charge. Any sheet metal or plumbing shop also can do the work.

Measure the distance between the assemblies (it should be 18 inches). Cut the pipe about ⅜ inch shorter than this distance to allow for adjustment. Thread a flange to each end of the pipe, and adjust them so that the overall length matches the distance between the posts. Use #12 × 1¼-inch flathead screws to secure the flanges to the posts.

Spread 6 to 10 inches of resilient material, such as bark chips, around the play area.

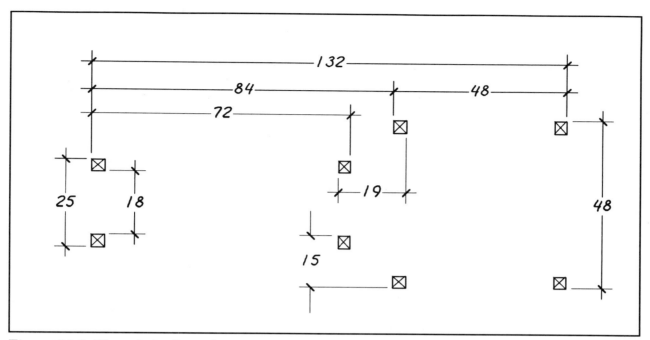

Figure 14.1. Plan view of post layout

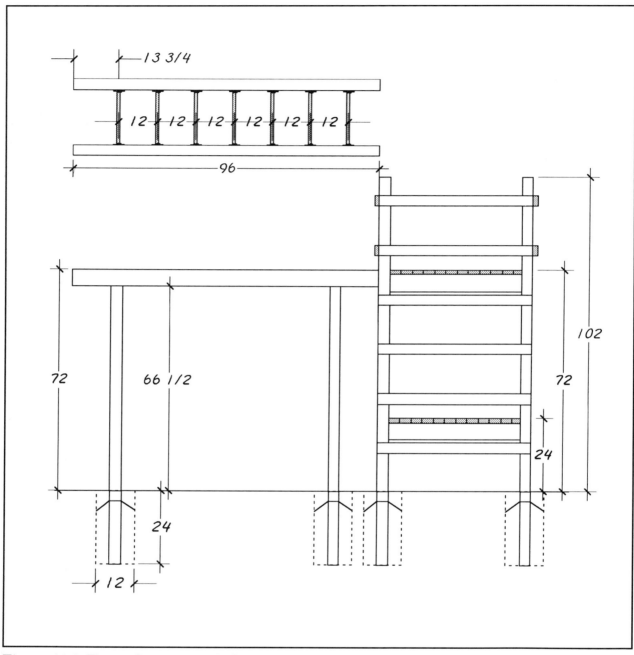

Figure 14.2. Front elevation and plan view of bar layout

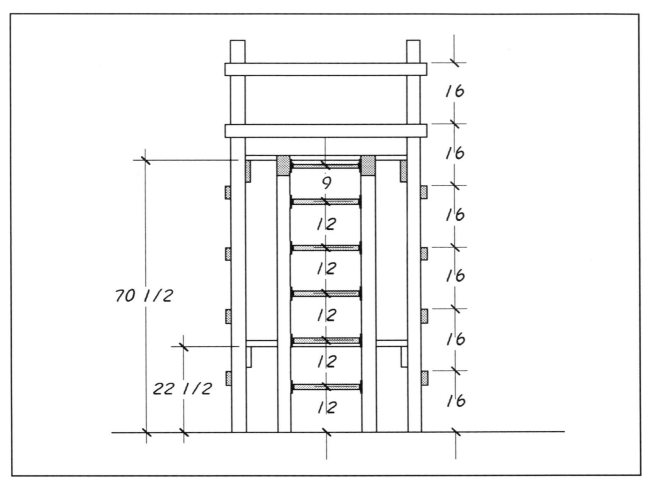

Figure 14.3. End elevation

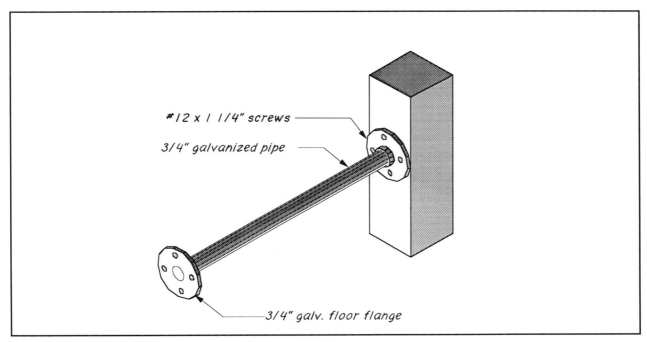

Figure 14.4. Detail showing bar and flange at post

· Project 15 ·
SUBURBAN

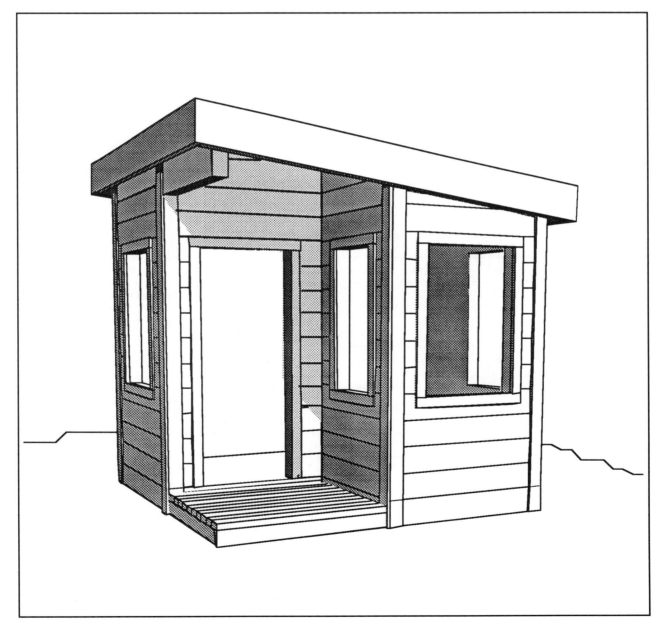

The Suburban's shallow ($1\frac{1}{2}$-in-12, 7-degree) shed roof covers 49 square feet, including a small porch nestled in the crook of the house's ell. The portion of roof that covers the porch is supported by a cantilevered beam.

BUILDING THE FLOOR

Carefully study the plans and materials list before beginning. Consider ground slope and other conditions to determine special foundation needs.

Refer to Figure 15.2 for the joist layout plan. Notice that the joists are spaced less than 24 inches on center. Assemble the floor as described in part 1.

BUILDING THE WALLS

Snap chalk lines 4 inches in from the perimeter of the floor. Cut and tack down the plates as described in part 1. The back wall and the two front walls each receive corner posts. The plates for the back wall are 83 inches, the frontmost wall $41\frac{3}{4}$ inches, and the door wall $44\frac{3}{4}$ inches. Cut the plates for the remaining walls to fit between these.

With the exception of the windows in the right-side wall, the openings are centered in their walls. The two openings are exactly opposite their counterparts in the shorter left-side walls.

Count the number of studs you will need, and cut them $67\frac{1}{2}$ inches long. Cut twelve trimmers $58\frac{1}{2}$ inches long. Each of the headers is 3 inches longer than its rough opening is wide. All headers can be single 2×4s. Cut the other pieces as needed.

There is no particular order in which you should build the walls. As you complete each wall, set it aside unsheathed. Erect the two long walls first, and nail them securely to the floor. Make sure the corner is plumb, then nail it together. Repeat the process for the other walls. Nail down the doubler plates as described in part 1.

Project 15 Materials List

Description	Quantity	Length in feet	Comments
4×4	2	8	Pressure-treated posts
2×6	7	8	Pressure-treated stringers, bridging
2×4	7	8	Pressure-treated porch components
2×4	36	12	Studs, trimmers, bottom chords
4×8	1	8	Beam
2×6	7	8	Rafters
1×8	4	8	Cedar fascia, rake molding
Pier blocks	8		
$\frac{3}{4}$" flooring	2		Sheets, treated
$\frac{1}{2}$" sheathing	7		Sheets
$\frac{3}{8}$" CCX	1		Sheet for soffit
Nails, screws			As needed

The roof rises 10 inches from one wall to the other. This rise is achieved with a 4×10 (actually $9\frac{1}{2}$ inches) and a $3\frac{1}{2} \times 47$-inch strip of $\frac{1}{2}$-inch sheathing. Put the plywood strip on the top of the frontmost wall first. Cut the 4×10 $83\frac{1}{2}$ inches long, and toe-nail it to the plate flush with the framing at the corner.

Next, nail the sheathing onto both load-bearing walls using 7d or 8d nails (galvanized if you will not be applying siding later) spaced 8 to 10 inches apart. It is most important that the sheathing tie the beam to the wall. For best results, use a full, unbroken sheet to provide maximum strength to the cantilevered beam.

BUILDING THE ROOF

The rafters are cut from 2×6 stock. Refer to Figure 15.5 for the length and seat cuts. The barge rafters are the same length as the others but have no seat cuts.

The rafters don't follow a consistent pattern. Place one directly over each gable (including over the door). Both of the remaining rafters are centered between the gables.

Toe-nail the rafters to the plate and beam, then cut short blocks to fill under the rafters at the gables and along the short wall opposite the beam (Figure 15.4). Sheath the remaining walls.

Nail lengths of 1×8 cedar to the rafter tails, using 8d galvanized nails. Center each fascia so that it runs wild past each gable end. Nail the barge rafters between the fascias. The outside face of each barge rafter is 5 inches from the wall. Trim the fascias flush with the barge rafters.

Nail on the roof sheathing and the 1×8 rake mold. Finally, cut pieces of $\frac{3}{8}$-inch plywood for the soffit under the eaves and the porch ceiling (Figure 15.3), and nail those in place.

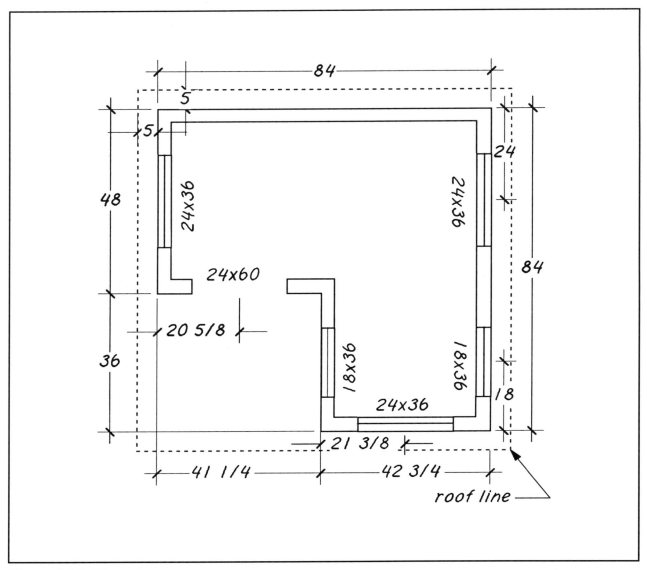

Figure 15.1. Plan view

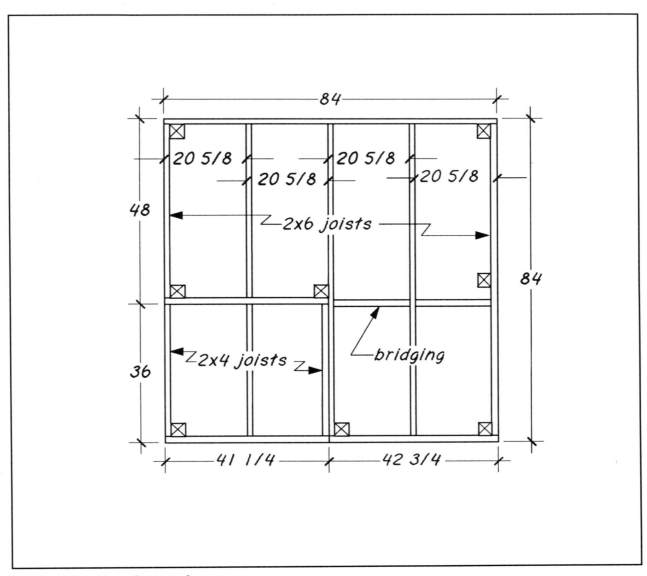

Figure 15.2. Foundation plan

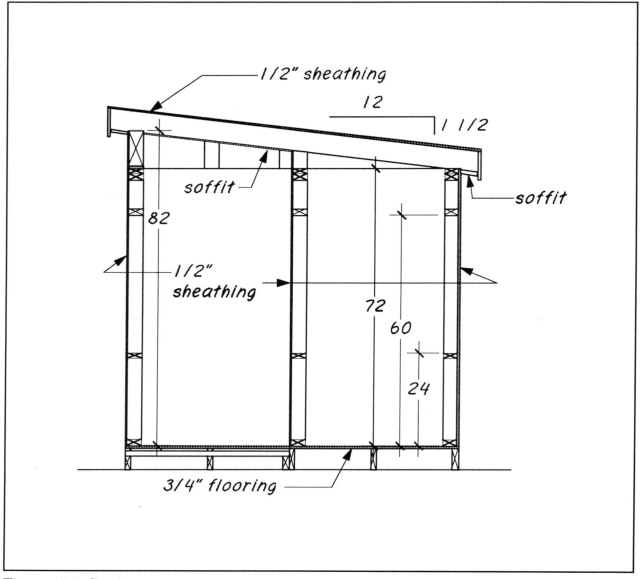

Figure 15.3. Section

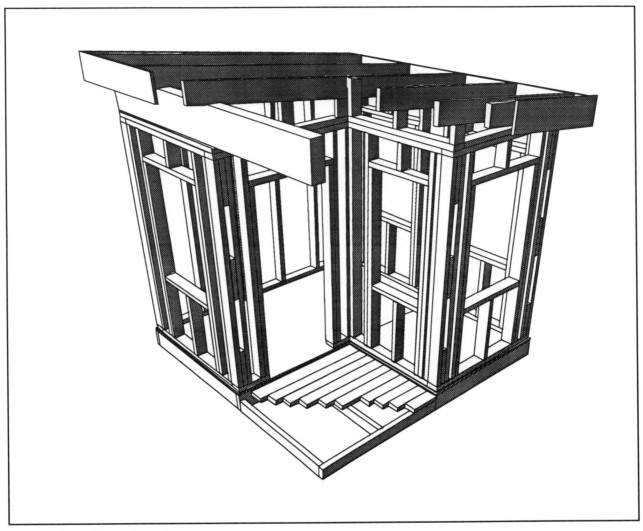

Figure 15.4. Framing plan

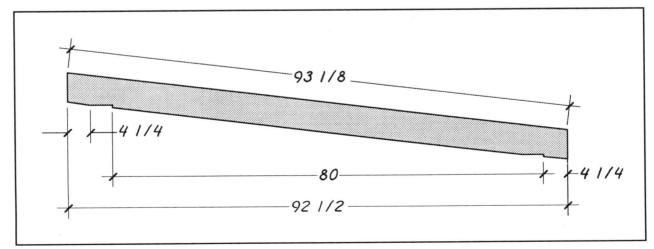

Figure 15.5. Rafter detail

▪ Metric Conversions ▪

INCHES TO MILLIMETRES

IN.	MM	IN.	MM
1	25.4	51	1295.4
2	50.8	52	1320.8
3	76.2	53	1346.2
4	101.6	54	1371.6
5	127.0	55	1397.0
6	152.4	56	1422.4
7	177.8	57	1447.8
8	203.2	58	1473.2
9	228.6	59	1498.6
10	254.0	60	1524.0
11	279.4	61	1549.4
12	304.8	62	1574.8
13	330.2	63	1600.2
14	355.6	64	1625.6
15	381.0	65	1651.0
16	406.4	66	1676.4
17	431.8	67	1701.8
18	457.2	68	1727.2
19	482.6	69	1752.6
20	508.0	70	1778.0
21	533.4	71	1803.4
22	558.8	72	1828.8
23	584.2	73	1854.2
24	609.6	74	1879.6
25	635.0	75	1905.0
26	660.4	76	1930.4
27	685.8	77	1955.8
28	711.2	78	1981.2
29	736.6	79	2006.6
30	762.0	80	2032.0
31	787.4	81	2057.4
32	812.8	82	2082.8
33	838.2	83	2108.2
34	863.6	84	2133.6
35	889.0	85	2159.0
36	914.4	86	2184.4
37	939.8	87	2209.8
38	965.2	88	2235.2
39	990.6	89	2260.6
40	1016.0	90	2286.0
41	1041.4	91	2311.4
42	1066.8	92	2336.8
43	1092.2	93	2362.2
44	1117.6	94	2387.6
45	1143.0	95	2413.0
46	1168.4	96	2438.4
47	1193.8	97	2463.8
48	1219.2	98	2489.2
49	1244.6	99	2514.6
50	1270.0	100	2540.0

The above table is exact on the basis: 1 in. = 25.4 mm

U.S. TO METRIC
1 inch = 2.540 centimetres
1 foot = .305 metre
1 yard = .914 metre
1 mile = 1.609 kilometres

METRIC TO U.S.
1 millimetre = .039 inch
1 centimetre = .394 inch
1 metre = 3.281 feet or 1.094 yards
1 kilometre = .621 mile

INCH-METRIC EQUIVALENTS

FRACTION	DECIMAL EQUIVALENT CUSTOMARY (IN.)	METRIC (MM)	FRACTION	DECIMAL EQUIVALENT CUSTOMARY (IN.)	METRIC (MM)
	1/64——.015	0.3969		33/64——.515	13.0969
1/32——.031		0.7938	17/32——.531		13.4938
	3/64——.046	1.1906		35/64——.546	13.8906
1/16——.062		1.5875	9/16——.562		14.2875
	5/64——.078	1.9844		37/64——.578	14.6844
3/32——.093		2.3813	19/32——.593		15.0813
	7/64——.109	2.7781		39/64——.609	15.4781
1/8——.125		3.1750	5/8——.625		15.8750
	9/64——.140	3.5719		41/64——.640	16.2719
5/32——.156		3.9688	21/32——.656		16.6688
	11/64——.171	4.3656		43/64——.671	17.0656
3/16——.187		4.7625	11/16——.687		17.4625
	13/64——.203	5.1594		45/64——.703	17.8594
7/32——.218		5.5563	23/32——.718		18.2563
	15/64——.234	5.9531		47/64——.734	18.6531
1/4——.250		6.3500	3/4——.750		19.0500
	17/64——.265	6.7469		49/64——.765	19.4469
9/32——.281		7.1438	25/32——.781		19.8438
	19/64——.296	7.5406		51/64——.796	20.2406
5/16——.312		7.9375	13/16——.812		20.6375
	21/64——.328	8.3384		53/64——.828	21.0344
11/32——.343		8.7313	27/32——.843		21.4313
	23/64——.359	9.1281		55/64——.859	21.8281
3/8——.375		9.5250	7/8——.875		22.2250
	25/64——.390	9.9219		57/64——.890	22.6219
13/32——.406		10.3188	29/32——.906		23.0188
	27/64——.421	10.7156		59/64——.921	23.4156
7/16——.437		11.1125	15/16——.937		23.8125
	29/64——.453	11.5094		61/64——.953	24.2094
15/32——.468		11.9063	31/32——.968		24.6063
	31/64——.484	12.3031		63/64——.984	25.0031
1/2——.500		12.7000	1——1.000		25.4000